withdrawn

The Complete
BEARDED
COLLIE

JOYCE COLLIS
AND PAT JONES

RINGPRESS

To the early breeders of the Bearded Collie, for keeping alive a breed that now gives so much pleasure to so many people, the world over.

RINGPRESS

Published by Ringpress Books Ltd,
Spirella House, Bridge Road,
Letchworth, Herts, SG6 4ET

Discounts available for bulk orders
Contact the Special Sales Manager at
the above address. Telephone (0462) 674177

First Published 1992
© 1992 JOYCE COLLIS AND PAT JONES

ISBN 0 948955 32 6

Printed and bound in Singapore
by Kyodo Printing Co

CONTENTS

FOREWORD

The amazing growth of popularity of the working breeds is one of the outstanding features of the second half of the century. Prior to that they were neglected by those interested in the 'pedigree' breeds. As recently as 1935 the number of breeds in the Working Group registered with the English Kennel Club was less than the totals for Hounds, Gundogs or Terriers. The registration figures followed a similar pattern throughout Europe. Interest in the working dog and particularly the pastoral breeds lagged far behind. Traditionally, those who had the time, leisure and money to enjoy sporting pursuits were also the educated classes. A great deal was written about hounds and gundogs, little or nothing about sheep and cattle dogs.

In Britain the working prowess of the Border Collie led to the decline and eventual loss of a number of regional breeds. They did not arouse the interests of conservationists and there has been no concerted move to revive or even recreate them, as has been the case in some European countries. However, one breed that was not lost was the Bearded Collie. Its survival depended on a relatively small number of shepherds, and its current popularity is due to its re-introduction into the show ring, where it eventually became a key breed in the growth of interest in the other long-coated pastoral breeds of Europe: the Briard, Puli, Komondor, Nizinny and the Bergamasque. The Beardie's handsome appearance, intelligence and lively affectionate nature, and its sound construction, led to the recognition of similar qualities in foreign breeds, originally created for work very similar to that of the Bearded Collie.

It is a paradox of the pedigree dog world that the very qualities which set off moves towards conservation, frequently come to work against a breed's best interests. It happens when exhibitor-breeders lose sight of the breed's essential balance, as they move away from its primary function, and exaggerate particular features at the expense of others. The Bearded Collie has come close to that point.

It is fortunate that at this crucial time, the authors of this book have collaborated. They have the essential authority of great experience and success in breeding and showing Bearded Collies, for their words to be valued. At least as important, however, is their understanding of a whole range of working breeds which they have owned, bred and shown. Between them they have a knowledge of the primary work of the pastoral breeds, and an appreciation of the principle of form following function, the practice of which is essential to the future of the Bearded Collie. They have the advantage of having seen and known dogs now recognised as pillars of the breed. Judging experience, which extends beyond the British Isles to the far countries where the Bearded Collie has become one of the most popular of breeds, provides a further force behind their writing. A one-to-one apprenticeship provides the ideal learning situation in which to pass on the knowledge of dogs accumulated over many years. It is rarely possible. I was delighted to be asked to write the Foreword to this exposition of the breed which has so much to offer, not only to newcomers, but to the authors' contemporaries in the breed, and to those who judge Bearded Collies without actually having owned them. It is the next best thing to a direct relationship with craftswomen.

Harry Baxter
International Championship Judge

INTRODUCTION

JOYCE COLLIS: BEAGOLD KENNELS

I have now been dedicated to breeding, showing and living with dogs for some thirty-five years. I began my association with dogs on my own in 1955, although we had always had a variety of different breeds as family dogs over the years. My chosen prefix Beagold comes from the Golden Retrievers and Beagles that I owned. It was in 1963 that I bought my first Bearded Collie from Mrs Banks of the Gayfield prefix – and my second bitch, Ch. Beagold Ella (Ch. Bosky Glen of Bothkennar out of Martha Scrope Of Swalehall), soon gained her Championship title. Jayemji Derhue was my first Beardie dog. I have always preferred dogs, so I kept Beagold Buzz, Beagold Buffer, and then Ch. Davealex Royle Baron, my beloved companion, pet and show dog, who quickly gained his title. I loved all my dogs, but Baron held a special place in my affection. When he died at fifteen and a half years of age I lost a dear friend, and I mourn him to this day.

A relation of Baron's was Ch. Edenborough Star Turn At Beagold, who was bought from Shirley Holmes when he was nine weeks old. He grew into a gorgeous, glamorous dog, who won sixteen Challenge Certificates and eleven Reserve CCs. On many occasions he came second to his famous sire, the world-renowned Ch. Edenborough Blue Bracken. Star Turn was used extensively at stud, and he sired many Champions. The most notable was Ch. Beagold David Blue, who was exported to Norway after he gained his title in Britain. He went on to become Int. Scan. Nor. Swed. English Ch. Beagold David Blue. He was joined by Nor. Swed. Ch. Beagold Billy Brown, Nor. Ch. Beagold Silver Mist, and David Blue's son, who later became Int. Ch. Scan. English Ch. Beagold Nikki Nort. Beagold Black Moses was exported to Holland and soon gained his title. He followed in the footsteps of Int. Dutch Ch. Beagold Bruin Scott. As there was so much demand for our stock, we thought it a wise move to import Nor. Ch. Twinklestar Extra Special Mix (Stefan), who was the sixth generation of our line in Norway, with David Blue on

Joyce Collis with Beagold Porter Harvey. This dog was exported to Denmark, where he was a highly successful sire.

both sides. I have judged extensively abroad, all breeds, but usually I am asked to include Bearded Collies in my classification. At the moment my partner and I are campaigning Border Collies. We owned the first Border Collie Champion, Sh. Ch. Tilehouse Cassius At Beagold, and have recently imported a blue dog from New Zealand. He is now Sh. Ch. Clan Abby Silver Kiwi At Beagold, having won eleven CCs and seven Reserve CCs. He has sired some beautiful puppies, who will be campaigned over the next few years.

PAT JONES: WELLKNOWE KENNELS

I have spent my life totally surrounded by animals for as long as I can remember. I have lived in the Lake District for the last twenty-five years and my greatest pleasure is being close to nature, and watching both bird and animal wildlife. My grandfather was a gamekeeper, so it is easy to see an example of type missing a generation and then reappearing in a very dominant way, in me!

I have spent thirty-five years as a professional animal trainer, and this has given me opportunities that many people only dream about. A love of animals has no barriers: and Kings, Queens and commoners can all share the same passion. Prize-winning rabbits, sheep, cattle, horses and goats have always interested me, and have been kept at Wellknowe, but now I concentrate on dogs. I have bred Champions in Bearded Collies, Border Collies, Shetland Sheepdogs, Skye Terriers, Lowchens and Belgian Shepherds (Tervuerens), in fact I sent the very first Tervueren into Australia, who went on to become the first Champion. I have also bred CC winners in Tibetan Terriers and Dobermans.

My dogs are now all basically show dogs, and I breed an occasional litter. At the moment I have four Bearded Collie Champions, three others with Reserve CCs, a CC winning Border Collie, a CC winning Skye Terrier and the non-CC breed, Portuguese Water Dogs. The Water Dogs have been winners of many awards, but the most satisfying is that they have won Top Stud, Top Brood, and Top Dog for the two years that the awards have been given. I am now very interested in judging, and this keeps me very busy in the UK and abroad. It is a truly marvellous experience to not only go and see superb dogs, but to have the chance to travel, to see the world and all its treasures.

Pat Jones winning Best of Breed with Ch. Wellknowe Shepherd Boy at Leeds Championship Show.

(Above) Cowherd in Co. Durham with his working Collie in 1901. By the Rev. James Pattison.

(Left) A farmer with his working sheepdogs in 1908. One dog is smooth-coated, the other is coated like a Bearded Collie.

THE PET LAMB.

Chapter One

HISTORY OF
THE BEARDIE

The origins of the Bearded Collie stretch back into distant time, and canine historians can only speculate as to its exact history. Kathryn Braund, writing in her book *Uncommon Dog Breeds* suggests that the Bearded Collie's ancestor, the Highland Collie, was brought into Britain thousands of years ago. It is widely believed that Central Asia was the birthplace of all the world's sheep, and so it is logical to assume that the dogs accompanied the old pastoral tribes as they migrated westwards. In those far-off days the dogs were used to watch over the flocks and herd them, as they moved across Europe. The dogs that travelled with the Iberians and Celts reached Britain and found a new home in the northern Scottish highlands.

In a document dated 1514 a Polish shipmaster, Kazimierz Brabaski, sailed to Scotland to trade grain for sheep. He carried six Polish Sheep Dogs, using them to move the sheep on and off his ship. The Scottish shepherds were so impressed with these useful dogs that they traded prize rams for three of the dogs. It is said that these dogs bred with the Highland Collie, and formed the foundation lines of the Bearded Collie. Another theory is that as sheep and cattle, accompanied by dogs, were moved all over the world during the Middle Ages, it is quite possible that Beardie's ancestors could have been the Russian Owtchaka, the French Chien de Berger de la Brice, or the old Welsh Gray, which is like a smaller Beardie. This type can also be seen in the Barbucho or Patagonia sheepdog. As many Welsh settlers lived in the Chubcett Valley and other parts of Patagonia, there is certainly a link with the old Welsh Gray. Clifford Hubbard, writing in his book, *Working Dogs of the World*, states that the Barbucho gets its name from the Spanish word for beard.

James Dalgliesh's book, *The Collie*, puts forward the possibility that the Bearded Collie is closely related to the Old English Sheepdog, as they both were found in Scotland. However, it is more likely that they were related as 'cousins', or dogs of a similar type, rather than any more intimate tie. There is an historic picture called *The Sheepdog* by Philip Reinagle, which is a typical Old English with a tail, which, if shown to a Scottish shepherd today, would be called a Bearded Collie. Gordon James Phillips of Glenlivet (Russell Greig, *The Bearded Collie*) states in a letter in the *Live Stock Journal*, 15th November 1878, that there is or was a strain of Beardies with a tail, which he describes as "a stump generally from six to nine inches". The Bearded Collie, known as the Highland Collie, remained secluded in the Highlands during the the late nineteenth/early twentieth century – a period when farmers were much occupied with finding and breeding good working dogs. As a result, the Beardie remained relatively pure, and the breed that originated many centuries ago forms the basis of all that we have today.

In 1912 Russell Greig MRCVS tried to bring the Beardie into prominence, and he formed The Bearded Collie Club in Edinburgh, but this foundered with the outbreak of World War One. In the thirties Mrs Cameron Miller bred and exhibited Beardies, but when she died, nothing was heard of the breed until the registration of Jeannie Of Bothkennar in 1948, and Bailie Of Bothkennar in 1949. Only a handful of people, and these were mainly farmers, kept Beardies in the war years. They were long-haired, hard to keep clean, and slower at work that the speedier, shorter coated, smaller Border Collies. Luckily some people did care, and it was only because of their untiring efforts that the Bearded Collie survived. The show-going Beardie owners are well acquainted with the wonderful work of Mrs G. O. Willison, whose prefix, Bothkennar, is behind all today's show dogs. Mrs Willison was determined to promote the breed, and in 1955 she enlisted the support of all her friends to make up sufficient numbers to form The Bearded Collie Club. Miss Clare Bowring was asked to become President, and the late Jimmie Garrow and the late Frank Williemas, together with various members of her family, made up the necessary number, all paying an enrolment fee of £2. However, it was not until 1967 that registrations with the English Kennel Club reached the magical figure of 150, and the breed could be officially registered. Crufts 1959 was the first time that Challenge Certificates were offered.

THE BOTHKENNAR STORY

Joyce (Collis) contacted Mrs Willison in the sixties in the hope that the great lady would write her story of the Bothkennar Beardies, but ill health made her reluctant to go ahead with this project. After repeated efforts she agreed to let Joyce interview her, and subsequently she used material from the interview in a book called *The Bearded Collie*. This, in Mrs Willison's own words, is her story.

"I was living at Bothkennar Grange, Sandy Lodge, near Northwood, Middlesex, when my first Beardie, Jeannie Of Bothkennar, came into my possession. She was obtained from a farmer's agent when she was two months old in January 1944, and she was registered in 1948. While I was exercising her on the golf course, opposite the house, a gentleman, who subsequently turned out to be a shepherd, admired Jeannie and tried to persuade me to part with her. I refused, and subsequently I wrote several letters to the previous owner of Jeannie, Mr Bruce Keith, asking him to find a male Beardie, and later on another bitch, but with no result. However, Jennifer Of Multan was bought from him some years later. Jeannie was not only the most obedient dog I

One of the few surviving photographs of Jeannie Of Bothkennar, taken in 1950. This bitch was the first Bearded Collie to be registered, and her bloodlines formed the foundation of the breed in Britain and overseas.

have ever owned, but without any training she could work all kinds of livestock, poultry, sheep, cattle and obstinate goats. She had 'the eye', and could control all my other dogs just by staring at them, and they would do just what she wanted. It was because of her wonderful qualities, her intelligence and her endearing nature, that I felt I must perpetuate her strain – so I set about trying to find her a mate.

"The Kennel Club was no help as there were no Beardies registered, and the farmer's agent who had sold her to me was unable to get me a male Beardie. However, when Jeannie was two years old, I saw a typical Beardie, but with parents unknown. The local dog shop thought his dam was a Border Collie. The two were mated and produced ten puppies, eight bitches and two dogs (one died at birth). The day after they were born, we removed three pups and let Jeannie rear only six. I had to go into hospital for a major operation when the pups were three weeks old. As soon as I recovered sufficiently from this I went away with my parents to convalesce, and on my return I found that my family had found 'good homes' for the five true Beardies, and left me only a Border throw-back. I was very upset, but consoled myself with the thought that I could mate the two again the following year. But this was not to be. The dog, who was about twelve years old when he mated Jeannie, died, and a month before Jeannie came into season, the surviving dog puppy died from distemper. I was determined to continue with my search to find a mate for Jeannie, and I had Collie breeders and farmers' agents all over England and Scotland hunting for another Beardie dog for me, but they were unable to find any that were pure-bred. (I paid out large sums in travelling expenses.) Eventually I found David, registered as Bailie Of

Bailie Of Bothkennar (left) and Bess Of Bothkennar, pictured with Wendy Willison.

Bothkennar, in September 1949. He was then aged sixteen and a half months, and although I was given the name of the farmer who had bred him, and the district he came from, I was unable to contact him as he had emigrated to South Africa, taking his dogs with him.

"Bailie and Jeannie were mated in 1950, and I kept the four best pups – three dogs, Bogle, Bravado and Bruce (the only brown), and the bitch, Buskie. The greys were all born black. (All those born blue grey that I had subsequently, I used "Blue" in their registered name.) The following year I mated Jeannie to Bruce, and it was a most tragic year. Jeannie gave me a large litter of browns, but two or three days later a dead puppy's head was found in her bed. I called in the vet and he said she must have eaten the body. All the original puppies were thriving. Two days later I went on holiday, leaving the dogs in the care of the kennelmaid. Then the puppies started dying, one by one. I was not told – they didn't want to spoil my holiday. When I was finally informed, there were only two puppies left, both dogs. I immediately phoned the kennelmaid with full instructions for putting them on the bottle, and the poor little starvelings picked up. The vet had not realised that the dead puppy left behind had caused an infection of the uterus, which dried up the milk supply. One of the puppies was exactly like Bruce; and the other, a replica of Jeannie, became the apple of my eye However, at six months old they caught an infection, which the vet said was a tummy upset – nothing serious. But a week later, one developed a choking cough, and although the vet said it was still nothing to worry about and gave me some cough mixture, I called in another vet; he said immediately that it was either hard-pad or distemper, and if they had been treated for it at the beginning they would have recovered. It was too late, and although the new vet did everything possible, we lost them.

"The same year a lady in Sussex heard about Bailie and brought up a superb Beardie bitch to be mated to him. Although she was eleven years old, the bitch conceived. However, she produced no puppies at the appointed time, and the local vet was called in. He was quite definite that she was not in whelp. A fortnight later she produced two dead puppies. The vet was called again, and after examining her, said there were no more inside her. But a week later she died and a post mortem showed another very decomposed pup in her womb.

"I was advised not to mate Jeannie again, as it might kill her. Knowing how intelligent she was, I decided to leave the decision to her. She decided against it and refused to be mated. At about the time Jeannie had her brown litter, some friends in Scotland found me a four-and-a-half-year-old bitch. She was called Bess by her previous owner, who was a shepherd, so I registered her as Bess Of Bothkennar. She had been working sheep in Scotland and they bought her, complete with a pedigree signed by the breeders. They said she was a beauty, but she was a typical working Beardie, with no quality about her at all. She was sent down to be boarded by my vet until I returned from my holiday. I mated her first to Bogle. The only bitch in the litter was Briery Nan, which I later sold to Mr Owen on breeding terms, to be mated to his dog, Newtown Blackie. She produced no bitches in her first litter, and only one in her second, when he had first choice. I regretted parting with her, particularly as he in-bred to such an extent that he eventually produced caricatures of the Beardies.

"After Bess had her first litter, she became terribly jealous of Buskie and fought her most savagely, so I had to part with her. I offered her on breeding terms to the lady in Sussex, who had lost her bitch so tragically. I next mated Bess to Bailie and had a most beautiful bitch puppy from her, with a wonderful temperament. I wanted to keep her myself, but unfortunately she had been booked from the time of the mating, and there wasn't another good bitch in the litter, so I had to part with her. This was Bond, the dam of Int. Ch. Bobby Of Bothkennar and Ch. Blue

Mrs Moore's Newtown Blackie: sire of Ridgeway Rob and Bremhill Betty, grandsire of Ch. Wishanger Barley Of Wishanger and Ch. Wishanger Barberry Of Bothkennar.

Bonnie. When Buskie (Bailie – Jeannie), was old enough, I mated her back to her sire and kept Blue Peter and Bra'Tawny. Tawny's one fault was that her legs were too short. Peter was a lovely dog, and I showed him when he was old enough. He was Reserve Best of Breed to his sire. However, the next morning he was found completely paralysed in the kennel. The vet thought that one of the other dogs must have jumped down from the upper bunk, and landed on him, and injured a vital part of his neck or spine. He only partially recovered, and we had to have him put down before we could find a suitable mate for him.

"Bra'Tawny produced nine pups in her first litter, the best of which was Bannock (sire of Blue Bonnie), who would have been a Champion, only we had no CCs then. He was Best of Breed at Crufts in subsequent years. The best bitch was Baidh, who was mated to Bravado, which resulted in the first British Champion, Ch. Beauty Queen. Beauty was the first reddish fawn I had had since Bruce, except, of course, for the litter I lost, and she bred two Champions in her first litter, Ch. Bravo and Ch. Bosky Glen Of Bothkennar. At this time a very wealthy American lady came over to see my dogs and bought two lovely dog puppies from Bra'Tawny's litter. She wanted to start the breed in America and took the two dogs to her farm in Connecticut. She offered me a very high price indeed for two bitches suitable for mating with them, but at that time I only had their litter sisters, their dam and grand-dam, and Jeannie. Before I was able to supply the bitches, the lady died. Her father offered to pay the cost of transporting the dogs back to me and the full six months quarantine, but I couldn't bear the thought of their long confinement in kennels, and asked if they could place them together on another farm. This was done and the new owner came to see me later. Bra'Tawny's second litter produced Ch. Barley and Ch. Barberry. About the time that Ch. Beauty Queen was born, a young farmer from Sussex was sent to me by the Kennel Club, wishing me to pass his reddish-sandy Beardie bitch for registration. This I had no hesitation in doing. Jennifer Of Multan was a real beauty, and as she was just starting her season he left her with me to be mated to Bruce. I was kindly offered pick of litter in lieu of stud fee. So once more there was an all brown litter and I took the bitch who later became Ch. Bronze Penny, the dam of Ch. Benjie, the grand-dam of Ch. Bravo Of Bothkennar and great grand-dam of Ch. Bracken Boy. This was the first year that fortune smiled

Swalehall Martha Scope (Ch. Swalehall John Scope – Swalehall Fiona): dam of Ob. Ch. Scapa and Ch. Beagold Ella. Owned by Mrs Morris

on me, after the very difficult times I had at the start. I was interested in Obedience training with Beardies, and someone who knew of my interest in the breed found Britt (Jock ex Mootie) chained up on a farm in Dumfrieshire. The Polish farm worker who owned him had no idea how to train him, so kept him chained in case he ran out on the main road. She got the man to agree to sell him and fixed a price, then in due course he was sent down to me. He was born in August 1955, and when I had him at nine and a half months he was not house-trained and he had both round and tape worms. He turned out not only to be my best Obedience winner but won two CCs and about seven Reserve CCs. He was bred by the head herdsman on the farm, his dam working cattle and his sire, from a neighbouring farm, working sheep. I received full particulars of him from the breeder who signed his registration form. My first exports were to the United States of America. My next export was Britt Of Bothkennar – Bra'Tawny's son, who went to Finland, where he became an International Champion, as did a bitch I sent out to the same man later. I have also sent other Beardies to Finland, Sweden, Holland, Italy, France (which later went with

Mr Green's Swalehall John Scrope (Bruce Of Bothkennar – Jennifer Of Multan).

their owners to the USA), South Africa and Thailand."

Unfortunately the pictures that have survived of Jeannie Of Bothkennar – Mrs Willison's foundation bitch – are not very complimentary. She appears straight in shoulder, and short of neck, with a very tousled brown coat. No doubt the texture of the coat is correct, but to those who are familiar with the flowing coat of the present-day Bearded Collies, the bitch must look like a foreign breed. Mr Green's John Scrope of Swalehall and Swalehall Fiona look very similar to Jeannie, which is not surprising as she is the grand-dam. The pair were mated, and in the litter they produced

Ch. Blue Bonnie Of Bothkennar, at twelve years of age. She went to the Osbornes when Mrs Willison disbanded her kennel.

Swalehall Fiona, pictured in 1958, looked very like her grand-dam, Jeannie Of Bothkennar

Swalehall Martha Scrope, dam of Ob. Ch. Scapa and Joyce's Ch. Beagold Ella. Martha was a very shaggy-coated Beardie, owned by Miss Morris. Benji Of Bothkennar has been featured in nearly all the written accounts of the Bearded Collie's history. He was litter brother to Blimber Of Bothkennar and sire of Ch. Bravo Of Bothkennar out of Ch. Beauty Queen Of Bothkennar. It was mentioned that Blimber's mouth was half an inch overshot, but with the shortage of stud dogs in the breed it must have been necessary to use him for his other good show points. Bailie Of Bothkennar was a heavy-type dog and was the first male to be registered with the Kennel Club. His photos show a lot of coat, and a very handsome strongly made head. He is the sire of Bruce Of Bothkennar, who looks a good shape, with the right texture of coat. He obviously carried the gene for brown from his dam, Jeannie. Because of the shortage of bitches, Mrs

Willison decided to mate Buskie Of Bothkennar to her sire Bailie Of Bothkennar. In the litter was brown Bra'Tawny Of Bothkennar, who was shorter on leg than any of the other Beardies, but her coat was straighter than that of her relatives, as seen in a picture taken in 1956. Bravado Of Bothkennar also had an overshot bite, and this must have been a great worry to Mrs Willison, who had no choice in breeding stock in those early days.

In 1963 Mrs Willison disbanded her kennels, and she must have been immensely pleased to find dedicated show people to carry on the Bothkennar name. She gave Ch. Bobby Of Bothkennar to her kennelmaid, who shortly left for South Africa, where the dog won seven more CCs. A Champion bitch was exported to South Africa as a young puppy, and she was brought to Bobby to be mated. They went on to produce CC winning progeny. In the UK, Mr and Mrs Osborne took Ch. Bravo Of Bothkennar (Blimber Of Bothkennar ex Ch. Beauty Queen Of Bothkennar), and Ch. Blue Bonnie Of Bothkennar (Bannock Of Bothkennar ex Bond Of Bothkennar). Mary Partridge had Ch. Wishanger Barley Of Bothkennar (Ridgeway Rob ex Bra'Tawny Of Bothkennar). Suzanne Moorhouse had Ch. Willowmead Barberry Of Bothkennar, litter sister to Barley. Shirley Holmes had Ch. Bracken Boy Of Bothkennar (Ch. Bravo Of Bothkennar ex Ch. Blue Bonnie Of Bothkennar). Bravo and Mary Partridge's Ch. Wishanger Cairnbahn were used extensively at stud, and with one or two exceptions, most of the dogs and bitches of today descend from their breeding.

Chapter Two

CHOOSING A PUPPY

All puppies are tremendously appealing and it is therefore virtually impossible to make an objective assessment when you are confronted with a litter of beautiful Beardie puppies. The most important point to be decided is whether the puppy is wanted for show or as a pet. In a breed such as the Bearded Collie the colour and markings are important features to note at an early stage, particularly if a show puppy is required. If there is a variety of colours in the make-up of the parents and the grandparents, there might be a mixture of colours in the litter, and although perfect markings are not essential, hopefully there will be no complete mis-marks. The perfectly marked puppies should be noted for future reference. Both sexes are welcome in a litter, but the majority of buyers want bitches; so if there are more bitches than dogs, there will be no problem to sell them. It is very difficult to assess a puppy's potential before it has reached six to eight weeks of age. There are some breeders who say that they can pick a puppy when it is still wet, but this means focusing all the attention on colour and markings, and not taking other important factors, such as movement and temperament, into account. In fact, Pat does not allow herself to be influenced by colour or markings, and she prefers to look for the pup that has the correct construction and a good head. The Wellknowe Beardies tend to be plain-coloured with minimal white markings. A considerable degree of skill and expertise is required to select a puppy for show, even when you wait until it is a little older. These are skills that should be acquired over a period of time.

It is a good idea to decide on the sex of the puppy that you are going to keep before the litter is born. In most pet homes this is largely a matter of personal choice – breeders and exhibitors may have other factors to take into account, depending on their kennel's breeding programme. However, if you already have one dog, and you want mixed sexes, you must be able to provide separate kennelling arrangements when the bitch comes into season. When you have made up your mind, and weighed all the pros and cons, stick to the decision you made when sanity prevailed, and do not get side-tracked when you see the litter for the first time. There are few

Farleycross Ankaret at eight weeks old. A very pretty blue bitch puppy, showing good ear-set, excellent eye-shape, and a sweet, feminine expression.

A litter of eight-week-old Beardie puppies, all looking equally appealing.

people who do not get carried away when they see a kennelful of beautiful Beardie puppies, and it is all too easy to throw caution to the winds and pick a puppy because 'it is cute', 'it has perfect markings', 'it is such a lovely colour', or, what usually happens, 'it looks at you with those lovely eyes'. If the puppy is to be kept as a pet, any of those reasons can be the one that makes you choose that particular puppy, but for the show ring, many other details need to be taken into consideration.

By three weeks the puppies have developed individual characters. There is the greedy black and white dog, who is always first to his mother's teat. There is the little blue bitch, a dainty little creature, who will be a glamour girl when she grows older, and with her lovely blue colour and dove grey-blue eyes to match, she will certainly be one of the first to go. There is the adventurous one, into all sorts of mischief, even managing to climb out of the whelping box, long before the others have attempted to leave the warmth and comfort under the heat lamp. There is the little fawn bitch, who, not so big as the others, is developing a gorgeous champagne colour as she grows older. She could well catch up in size, but being so small, she is sometimes pushed out in the scramble for the best teat. This is the one that will need extra food when it comes to weaning. At the opposite extreme there is the brown bitch, a fat, roly-poly happy, little creature, no trouble to anyone as she eats and sleeps most of the time.

By the time they are five weeks old, the puppies are growing fast, and they should give all the indications that they are being fed enough and thriving nicely. If you have bred the litter yourself, you will have the opportunity to observe the puppies right up to the time when they are ready to go to their new homes, at between eight and ten weeks. This gives you the chance to watch and handle the puppies, and to learn about their different characteristics. If you are

Farleycross Action Man at six weeks old. A black and white dog puppy, showing excellent coat length and texture, plus the strong head that is needed in a male puppy.

looking for a show puppy, it is important to weigh up all these factors before making your final choice. If you have some knowledge of the sire and dam, and the grandparents, it is fairly easy to know what type of pups will result from the combination, especially if the litter is closely line-bred, or even inbred. Definite characteristics can be noticed, and although to the novice the puppies may appear to be evenly matched – every one a potential Champion – closer inspection will reveal a slight difference in the shape of the head, a different length of back, good and bad angulation, so that even with a line-bred litter careful study is needed. It is no good being litter-blind and regretting your choice later. Remember the points that you were looking for when the litter was planned: was there anything to improve or anything to correct from the sire and dam? Look at the puppies and discover where their strengths and weaknesses lie. If you are buying a show puppy, rather than selecting one from your own breeding, seek the advice of the breeder, who will have the experience to select a good puppy and will have a thorough knowledge of the puppy's bloodlines. In nearly all cases the breeder will be only too anxious to help you to select a top-class puppy; it is not in their own interests to send out a puppy from their kennel that is not a worthy specimen of the breed. Joyce's method of selecting a show puppy is to stand the puppy on a table, away from the rest of the litter, and check on the shape of head and length of neck, and make sure the topline is level. With experience and knowledge of previous litters, she checks that the head is a good shape, with the muzzle nice and square; and the teeth should be neither overshot or undershot, even at this age. Some breeders claim that the mouth will right itself, but she believes it is far better to eliminate this as a potential problem area at an early stage. Good ear-set at six to eight weeks of age will continue into the dog's adult life, and Joyce likes the ears to be large and set low. If the puppy is born black and white, there are very seldom pigment problems, or eyes which are too light in colour. In fact, very few breeders these days consider light eyes a fault, even though the Breed Standard states: "Eye to match coat colour". Joyce then feels the shoulder blades and the angle at which they reach the withers. The topline must be firm, with the tail set correctly. A high-set tail in a puppy will present a problem with the tail carried over the back when the dog is an adult. A breed as outgoing and friendly as the Bearded Collie is inclined to raise its tail on the move, so it is preferable to use stock with correctly set tails, so eliminating another problem. Forequarters must be straight: there should be no evidence of a 'ten to two' stance, as this is always apparent, even with the adult length of coat. This stance can also be caused by a narrow chest, which is undesirable in Bearded Collies. Joyce looks for a good bend of stifle, with a nice length of hock, as hocks that are too short give a foreign look to a Beardie. Pat looks for a balanced head, and well-laid shoulders with long upper arms. She likes to see a good length of rib, correct hindquarters and low hocks. She likes to be confident that the puppy has enough bone to develop correctly, and that it has a pleasing temperament.

At different stages of growth the Beardie puppy does look odd, and in no way does it resemble the beautiful show dog that you visualised. All you need is patience. Inexperienced owners may despair, but all puppies go through different stages. At four months its head could look narrow, and its ears could lift. In some cases the mouth may be overshot, though this should start to correct itself when the puppy is five-and-a-half to six months of age. However, the puppy could look completely different by the time it is nine months of age. If it does not alter for the best, the owner must remember that it is not the end of the world that the ugly ducking has not become a swan. It still has the makings of a loving pet, and if you are still determined to have a show dog, you will have learnt from the experience, and you will probably have better luck next time.

Chapter Three

TRAINING

There are basic rules that the new owner should abide by when bringing an eight-week-old puppy into the home. It should be remembered at all times that it is an animal, and it should be treated as such. It must be given love, good feeding and plenty of attention, but it is wise to remember that bad behaviour, such as biting, barking incessantly or wildness, will become a habit if it is not immediately corrected. What seems amusing in a naughty puppy will not be so funny when the puppy becomes an adult. It is no use allowing the puppy to misbehave and saying that you will correct it when it grows up; by then it is usually too late. The dog will look to its owner as leader of the pack, and it will respect and obey commands, right from the beginning, if they are given as commands – not as requests. Never allow a young puppy to bite your fingers, or play-bite your children. If it is getting too boisterous, distract it from the bad habit by giving it a toy to play with, or, if necessary, putting it in its bed (or wire cage) until it has calmed down. Children should never be allowed to play boisterously with a young puppy, as it will only get the puppy over-excited. It is better to allow children to play with the puppy under supervision, and then everyone will learn the correct behaviour.

Another basic rule is not to allow the young puppy the complete freedom to roam all over the house, especially if the owner is house-proud. When damage is done and there are puddles on the carpet, the poor puppy is banished from the centre of family activity to a remote part of the house. After having had complete freedom, it is no wonder that the puppy cries and wants to be let out. It is important to start off as you mean to go on, and restrict its territory. The puppy should be allocated an enclosed area where it is allowed to play, sleep and feed, with paper on the floor so that it can do its toilet. This is necessary at first, particularly if the weather is bad. When you start house-training, carry the puppy out into the garden or yard (which must be securely fenced) and take it to the same part of the garden on every occasion, and wait until it has relieved itself. It will soon learn to associate this particular place with being clean.

The breeder will have had a strict routine of feeding times, and the new owner should also try to feed at the same time every day. The puppies have built-in clocks and will expect to be fed at certain times. If an erratic timetable for feeding is adopted, then this is when trouble starts. The puppy goes past being hungry and will eventually lose interest in its food. This seems to be the reason why so many owners complain about their young adults not eating, and consequently being very thin. Good wholesome food is then wasted, and the owner resorts to giving the dog titbits at odd times. This is a sure ruination of any further attempts to have a good, sound, healthy dog.

Pat starts lead-training when the puppy is seven weeks of age, when she finds the pup has an intense will to please. As a result, lead training is merely an extension of following its owner's feet. This can be done in the house or in the garden until the puppy receives its first injection, which is usually at around twelve weeks of age, when the puppy can venture into the outside world. The first step is to attach the collar and let the puppy run around. Try to take the puppy's mind off the collar by playing. When it accepts the collar, attach a light lead to the collar and let it run around with the lead trailing. Continue to take its mind off the collar and lead. Then hold the lead, and go with the puppy wherever it wants to go; do not attempt to try to control the puppy at this stage. If it sits down, let it stay down; if it pulls against the lead, allow the lead to go slack. All you have to do is wait patiently until it moves, and then go with it. The next step is to get someone to call the puppy, let the puppy go to the caller, and then encourage it to walk back to where it was. This exercise can be repeated and made into a game, which the puppy will enjoy. A titbit will make the game even more interesting. A few minutes training each day is sufficient to begin with, and this can be built up gradually as the puppy starts to co-operate and walks nicely on the lead. After each lesson take the collar and lead off the puppy, and start afresh the next day. The collar and lead will then be associated with a walk. By the time the puppy has had all its injections, which is usually at about four months of age, and it is allowed to be taken out for a proper walk, your initial lead training should have paid off, and the dog should be a pleasure to walk with. If a young dog pulls against the lead, turn around and go the other way. If it pulls again, turn around and go back from whence you came. If necessary, repeat this exercise until the dog gives in, and stays by your side. This method invariably works, as the dog eventually realises that it is a waste of time to pull if you are not going anywhere.

When you are giving your dog a free run, in the park or in the country, recall it from the same spot on every occasion, and the dog will get used to coming back at this stage and being put back on the lead. The lead should never be used to hit the dog or it will remember the incident and will never come back when it is called. Do not allow a young dog to walk off the lead on the road, no matter how perfectly trained the dog is. You can never predict a loud noise or something else that may unsettle the dog, and unfortunately, there are far too many accidents that are caused by dogs running in the road.

Joyce remembers an incident many years ago, when she helped a friend to take six sows along a country lane to another field in the next village. The friend had trained her Collies to jump in the hedge as soon as they heard traffic. The party of dogs, sows and ladies set off early in the morning so that there would be no cars passing, and as it was raining they did not imagine that anyone else would be using the road. They had travelled about half a mile, when a car came along. The dogs jumped in the hedge, as they had been trained to do, but that left the huge sows free to wander. The occupants of the car must have been amazed to see two ladies dressed in old raincoats and six sows on the road – plus four dogs sitting in the hedge! They beckoned the car on, only to meet more traffic further up the road. This time the sows went off into a field, and the dogs ignored them, staying in the hedge, and taking no notice of the shouts and commands to fetch the sows. Joyce and her friend had to beg the car-drivers to proceed, explaining that the dogs would not come out of the hedge until they had passed. Tired, and extremely wet, they eventually reached the field where the sows were to stay, and the gate was firmly shut on them. On the long walk home they discussed the most sensible way of training dogs *not* to go into a hedge when traffic came past!

All dog owners run into problems when they are training, but the best policy is to stick to the basic rules, and start at the beginning as you mean to go on. A well-behaved dog is a happy dog; but perhaps more importantly, a well-behaved dog has a happy owner.

TRAINING FOR THE SHOW RING

The early training for show puppies is the same as for pet puppies, with one major exception. Right from the beginning show puppies should be encouraged to stand on

It takes time and patience to teach basic obedience.

command, never to sit. "Staaaaand" is the command that they get used to. When the puppy is in the correct position, it should get used to someone gently going over it, from head to tail. The usual practice is to start at the head, look in the mouth, and then combine stroking and feeling for shoulder placement, backline, curve of croup and tail set. If it is a dog puppy, it must get used to being checked to see if it is entire. A puppy that gets used to being handled and felt, will not present any problems when the judge goes over it in the show ring. When judging, it is easy to see dogs that have never had hands go over them, and as they grow older it is harder for them to adjust to a stranger approaching closely, let alone to allow intimate handling.

There are so many methods of showing the Collie. Some owners prefer to stack their dogs by placing their feet in position, then holding up the head and tail. If the dog is allowed to lean, this becomes a habit and the dog relies on the handler to hold it up, and with complete surrender to this method of handling, it sags in the middle, showing a weak topline. Alternatively, the handler lifts the dog up by a hand under the stomach, and with this method of stacking, the dog develops a roach back. Other owners prefer to train their Beardie to free-stand, using bait to keep their dog's attention. Everyone has their own methods, but the Bearded Collie is probably shown to best advantage when it is standing on its own, in front of the handler, with just a little check with the lead. This is, of course, when it has been trained to behave and show off its natural stance to the judge, and all the hard work at home will prove to be worth it. It is best to use a show collar

A basketful of puppies sired by Am. Ch. Arcadia's Cotton-Eyed Joe out of Am. Ch. Edenborough Quick Silver – five became Champions.

and lead when training the dog for the show, as well as in the show ring. The dog soon learns that the show lead means that it has to concentrate and work seriously for a short time. The leather collar and lead means that it is going out for pleasure.

When the judge approaches in the show ring, give the dog a few words of encouragement. While its head is being examined, you can reassure the dog by a gentle steadying of the lead. As the judge goes to the side and checks the rest of the dog, the handler should go back to hold the head. The dog does not know the judge, and it has every right to resent this stranger's approach. A seasoned show dog is familiar with the procedure, but a newcomer may well be nervous. This situation is often exacerbated by a novice exhibitor, who holds the lead taut, and allows the dog to lean. This has the opposite effect from reassuring the dog: it makes the dog more frightened of the stranger, and it probably senses that its owner is nervous and ill at ease. In this situation, Joyce, as a judge, feels that she should intervene. She tells the handler to move the dog up and down the ring, and then to come back and stand close to her, so that she can let the dog smell her hand. She then asks the owner to do a triangle, coming back to stand close to her, again letting the dog smell her hand. Then she gently pats the dog on the back, very gently at first, and strokes the dog down the back, assessing its topline, tail-set and the rear. By this time, with gentle handling, the dog relaxes and stands at ease, when it receives the command "stand" from the handler. Lastly, Joyce puts her hand to the dog's nose, and gently holds the head and quickly looks into the mouth. The handler is still standing back from the dog, but holding the lead. A mistake that is often made by handlers is to bend to look at the dog's mouth at the same time that the judge is attempting to do so. Of course, this just leads to problems for the judge, and the handler should stand back to give the judge a clear view.

If a dog is just nervous of being handled, usually in the Puppy Class, Joyce perseveres, but if any aggressive behaviour shows up she does not go any further with her examination. She just tells the owner to move the dog up and down in a triangle, but the dog will not be placed in the winner's line up. Some judges will send the dog out of the ring for this type of behaviour. However, whatever the judge's personal reaction might be, the owner should be aware that the judge has a difficult job to do, without having to cope with a dog that might bite. The temperament of most Beardies is excellent. They might be considered a bit boisterous and to need firm handling, but aggression is very rare. It is another very good reason why a puppy that tries to chew fingers, and jumps up to tug at a skirt or trouser leg, should be chastised immediately, before it develops into something more serious. If two dogs take an instant dislike to one another in the ring, Joyce, as judge, would send the pair to opposite corners of the ring. She recalls watching a ring full of Bearded Collies being judged, and when this situation occurred, one dog and handler were told to leave the ring, while the other went on to be awarded Best of Breed. In fact, both dogs were equally to blame, and they should have received equal punishment.

A Bearded Collie looks at its best when it is allowed to stride out on a loose lead. If a dog is strung up on a lead – whatever the breed – it produces an unnatural gait. When a Beardie is strung up it short-steps, and sometimes even has a mincing gait. Some handlers even hold out a ball or titbit in front of the dog, and this makes it move sideways, with stilted, high-stepping action. The movement of nearly all the Bearded Collies, whether inside a hall or outside on grass rings, is most typical of the breed when the dog is allowed to gait on a loose lead. The head is carried level with the body, the topline is level, and the tail is carried down to balance the body.

Training a Beardie to keep its tail down, or level with its back, is difficult with such a lively and friendly animal. It is a good idea to start working at this at a very early stage. Stay with the puppy when it is being fed and stroke its tail down all the time. As the pup grows older, let it play with a broom, and it will have to keep its tail down in order to maintain its balance. When the dog is walking on the lead, let it go a little in front and use a twig to gently hold the tail down. The dog will soon get into the habit of keeping its tail down, and it certainly helps if it fails to produce sufficient muscle to hold up its tail over its back. Some dogs are trained to respond to the word "Tail", and will keep it in the correct place in the show ring. In most instances, a low-set tail is always held correctly, but a high-set tail can be brought up as soon as the dog is on the move, completely spoiling the outline. Some Beardies hold their tails in a spring-like curl when they are moving; this does not look so bad, as long as it is is held down or level with the back.

When a dog is being assessed for movement, it should not need to be sent off round the ring (sometimes a very large ring) six or seven times. If the movement of the dog cannot be assessed after the second time round, especially if the dog has already done a triangle up and down, then the judge can only be testing the stamina of the handler. The breed is well-known for endurance – it can go all day and not tire; twenty times round the ring would show nothing different in the

Felix Cosme handles Ch. Beagold Fortune Beck so that he stands well and looks alert and interested.
                                                                    Dave Freeman.

dog's gait, but it would show that the human companion was out of condition and ready to drop!

The judge should keep in mind the whole time that this is a working dog par excellence. It must look as if it could do a day's work if called upon to do so, and therefore construction resulting in soundness should come before type. Minor faults, such as one or two premolars missing, should not be over-penalised if everything else is correct, but a dog that has an overshot or undershot mouth should not be placed. The owner will know by the time a puppy reaches the show ring that the dog's permanent teeth have grown correctly. If the mouth is overshot or undershot, or if it has developed a wry mouth, there is no point in continuing to show the dog or breeding from it. Very few judges will place a dog with one of these faults, which can be seen at a very early age.

Unfortunately, there is another mouth fault that can be seen in some Beardies. At the puppy stage the teeth go up into the top gums when the bottom jaw is narrower than the top jaw. When the bite is opposite, the baby teeth go into the bottom gums, making very sore holes that can get impacted with food. The baby teeth fall out, and, as the jaw is badly formed when the adult teeth grow, the dog cannot shut its mouth and its tongue usually hangs out. It is a very sad situation, when an otherwise good quality dog has this bad fault, which can be passed to its offspring.

When the judge has looked at all the dogs, the winning line-up will be selected. If you are placed, is important to remember that until you have the prize card in your hand, your performance is still not finished. The judge has to write a critique, and the dog should be standing still for this final assessment. The majority of judges find it most annoying when the winner encourages his dogs to give a wild performance to celebrate the win, before leaving the ring, forgetting that the judge is also writing a critique on the second and third dog, who could easily be upset by the abandoned behaviour of the winning dog and handler.

TRAINING CLUBS

Dog owners in Britain and America are lucky in having a great variety of dog activities to choose between, from Obedience classes, Agility and Show training to Judging Seminars and Working Test training. Therefore there is no reason for Bearded Collie owners to go to a show without first attending some training sessions with their dogs; and yet how often you hear an exhibitor say: "This is the first show, so he is not used to being handled" – and this could be at a Championship show, where the owner must know that nearly all the dogs will have been trained, and more than likely will have started in the smallest shows, before advancing to the important Championship shows. The Beardie needs training for the show ring. It is a very friendly and active dog, and with the slightest encouragement, it will make a fool of its owner by its lively behaviour. This can all be altered if the puppy is taken, when he is six months old, to a training school for show. The Obedience classes are not really ideal for a puppy that is going to be shown, for two reasons: the Obedience people are keen and dedicated to their sport, and if you are going to show your dog you do not want it sitting every time you halt; and having done Obedience in my early days, I know that dedicated Obedience people do not have patience with the members who have to have special instructions and commands so that their dog stands on command. An adult dog can go on to be trained for Obedience, as well as trained for showing, but it could confuse the puppy. It is better to start off with show training, and the Obedience can come later. Obedience Ch. Scapa was a show dog and an Obedience dog, but her owner, Jenni Wiggins, was an expert trainer and exhibitor in both fields of sport.

There are some very good training schools, usually organised by the Breed Clubs, and these are located in nearly all towns. The lessons are usually held in the evening, and can be for a six months course. A good starting point for a young dog is to compete in matches, which are staged by local canine societies. The dog usually enjoys this first attempt at competing with other dogs at a friendly meeting, where one dog competes against only one other, until the winner has beaten them all.

It takes time and patience to train your dog for the show ring, but it is worth every minute when you walk into the ring with the confidence that your dog will perform perfectly, and you can be justly proud of your joint performance.

Chapter Four

GROOMING

THE PUPPY

The Bearded Collie puppy does not have a long coat until it is about four months old, but it is most important to start getting the pup used to the brush and comb and to having its teeth cleaned and ears attended to, right from the beginning. A couple of times a week put the puppy on the grooming table and brush its coat, taking out any tangles with the comb. Make this a pleasant time for the puppy: talk to it and make a fuss of it while you are attending to its physical well-being. The teeth should be cleaned very gently with a soft brush and using special canine toothpaste, which is readily available. Ears should be inspected regularly, and gently cleaned with cotton wool (cotton) dipped in warm water, so it is damp. The Bearded Collie tends to grow hair in the ears, and this needs to be plucked out so that it does not collect wax and dirt. Nails need to be clipped with nail clippers, and it is especially important to keep a check on the dewclaws so that they do not become too long, catching on things, which could hurt the pup. (Some breeders avoid this problem by having the dewclaws removed from the puppy when it is a couple of days old.) This is the weekly attention every puppy must have, so that when it grows older it will accept the whole grooming process and enjoy the time it spends with its owner.

As the dog grows older, the coat grows longer, and all the puppy training on the grooming table becomes a necessity for the older dog. The correct amount of exercise on a hard surface will keep the claws short, but they should be checked regularly, and cut with the nail clippers so that they do not split. The feet must be inspected – underneath and between the pads, where the hair and mud may turn into a hard ball and be very uncomfortable for the dog to walk on. Some hair may be removed from across the eyes – maybe only a few strands. The lashes grow long and hold the hair up away from the eyes, but sometimes the hair grows quite thickly on the bridge of the muzzle and this can make the eyes sore. The hair around the dog's private parts can also be cut away: this saves it from getting wet, smelly and sore. The anus can also be kept clear

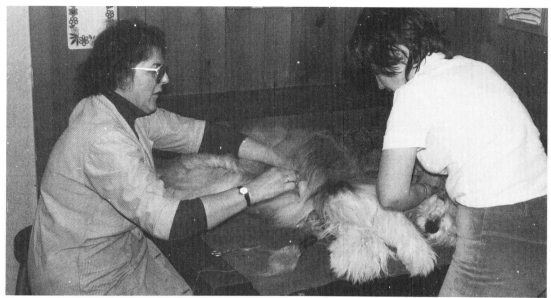

A grooming session in progress.

Styles of grooming have changed over the years: Modern presentation of grooming.

(Right) If the hair is over-plucked around the eyes it gives a harsh expression.

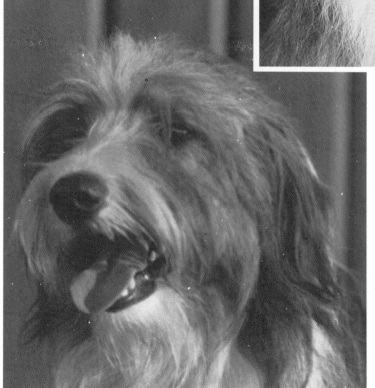

(Left) 1970 presentation of grooming.

so that it is easy to wash. All these grooming tips are for the pet dog as well as the show dog; both must be regularly attended to, including bathing and tidying-up the coat. Cosmetic alteration of the coat is taboo for the show ring, but when it is performed for the health, comfort and cleanliness of the dog, it is perfectly legitimate.

Newcomers to the breed should always be advised about the grooming that a Beardie will require, and the time and patience that is needed to perform this task on a regular basis. It is all too easy to fall in love with a Beardie puppy, and fail to realise that you do not have the time to take proper care of it when it becomes an adult with a long coat. Many years ago Joyce had a young dog, who had been sired by one of her stud dogs, returned by the owner. The dog was in a terrible state: his coat was matted all over his body, his ears stuck out at right angles, and he had matts of hair on the outside and the inside of his ears, with filth accumulated inside the drum. He had matts under his legs, and when he was groomed, wire was found entangled in the matts. He could only open his mouth slightly, as his beard was tangled in the hair falling from the bridge of his nose. This is an experience that every responsible breeder should learn from: you can never be too fussy when selecting homes for your puppies.

THE SHOW DOG

Pedigree dogs can be shown when they reach six months of age, and so a considerable amount of care and expertise is necessary if the show points of a Beardie are to be exhibited to its best advantage. A well-groomed, well-trained dog is much more likely to catch the judge's eye, than one that has had a brush five minutes before it is taken into the ring, and nothing has been done at home to prepare the dog for the show. Most serious exhibitors present their Beardies in immaculate condition. It is always obvious when hours of preparation have been spent grooming before the dog was brought to the show. It is always advisable to bath the dog seven days before the show, but some exhibitors bath either a couple of days or the day before the show, and consequently, the soft coats that can be seen in the ring can be a result of bathing rather than of breeders knowingly breeding for soft coats on their dogs. Rubbing the dog dry with a towel after a bath encourages growth, but many people rely on electric hair-driers, or if it is a hot day they allow the dog to dry in the sun.

Every day from bath-day to the day of the show, the coat should be brushed. This encourages the natural oils to return to the coat, and brings out a lovely shine. Time must be set aside so that the grooming session is not a rush job. The first essential is to make sure that the dog is in a comfortable position lying out on a grooming table. Then brush the coat in all directions, right down to the undercoat, using a top-quality wire hair-brush, such as a Mason Pearson brush, as this will not pull out the undercoat. There are other wire brushes available, but these are much too harsh for the Beardie coat and should never be used. The only time a comb should be used is to remove any tangles that might have formed under the chin, behind the ears, under the legs, around the feet or around the rear of the dog. The best comb to use is one made of steel, with rounded teeth. The dog should then be turned over to brush the other side. The next step is to get the dog to stand up, and to brush the coat down. However, the dog usually shakes as soon as it is allowed to stand, and the coat falls into place. The hair should be combed up and away from the eyes, so that it falls down, mingling with the hair on the ears. The beard should be combed forward – and make sure there are no tangles or food left around the mouth. Brush the hair on the legs and on the hocks upwards, and this will make it fall into place. If the coat is dry, use a lanoline coat spray. The Beardie should not have a parting put in from nose to tail; just let the coat fall into place in a natural parting. It looks completely unnatural to see a dead-straight parting, and there are few judges who will believe that it has fallen 'naturally' into place. A rub of chalk will bring up the white markings, but any chalking must be done at home and brushed out completely, as it is a Kennel Club rule that no chalk or powder must be left in a dog's coat when it is being shown.

On the day of a show it might be necessary to wash the feet and beard again, or to use a dry shampoo if the weather has been wet. Bad weather is a nightmare for Bearded Collie exhibitors. After all the preparation, it is heartbreaking for Beardie owners to see all their hard work ruined as the dog makes it way over muddy or wet ground from the car park to the showground. Many exhibitors now buy mackintosh leggings to protect their dog's legs, and many also use a cage for their dog on show days. This is usually fitted up so that the dogs can also be groomed on top of the cage. Then, when judging is over, the dog can be put in the cage, out of harm's way and can rest in comfort. It seems that more and more paraphernalia has to be taken to the dog shows for the Bearded Collie: brush and comb; towel, blanket, coat spray, lead and collar, show lead and collar, water bowl, food, if it is a long day – and that is just for the dog!

THE VETERAN

When the Beardie becomes a veteran, some dogs look no different and behave no differently. Others show their age and slow down. As they get older many lose their undercoat, but they still like to spend time being groomed. Nails must still be cut and eyes and ears regularly attended to. When a dog is over twelve years of age, the coat often has particles of dust, which are like dandruff, and no amount of brushing will get rid of them. A wise move is to cut the coat around the feet and all over the body, so that it is about two inches long. This keeps the dog cool in the summer and protects it for the winter, without having to bath the old dog. There will be Beardie owners who say that, as their dogs do not lose their undercoat, they will have no need to cut the coat. Everyone has their own ideas, but it appears that older dogs do appreciate less coat and seem to enjoy the extra freedom that this affords.

Chapter Five

HOUSING

The Bearded Collie adjusts quite happily to living in kennels or living in the house. There are few pet owners that need to kennel their dogs, but obviously the need arises if you are keeping a number of dogs. Most breeders have their own ideas and preferences with regard to the type of kennels that are suitable. The overall plan does not differ radically, but it is interesting to note individual ideas and then evaluate them accordingly.

At Joyce's Beagold kennels, the emphasis is on space and comfort. The kennels are constructed to give the maximum amount of comfort for the dogs to sleep in at night, and to have an exercise run for the day. The sleeping quarters measure approximately eight feet by twelve feet, with a bench for sleeping on, measuring two feet by two and a half feet, and 40 inches high. This amount of enclosed space is provided so that the dogs still have room to move about if the weather is bad, even on the worst days. However, on most days the door to each run is open, and the dogs can choose whether they want to be inside or outside. Fresh water is available at all times by means of a water dish, nailed to the wall, which prevents the dogs from spilling it. Each dog has an exercise run area measuring eight feet by sixteen feet, surrounded by a seven foot high wire fence. These large kennels and runs are designed to be as labour-saving as possible. In a show kennel absences are frequent, either because of going to shows as an exhibitor, or because of judging appointments, and so it it important that the person who comes to look after the kennels has only the minimum amount to do. The kennels are cleaned out daily, and while this is being done the dogs can play in the centre run, which measures about thirty feet square. Each dog is exercised every day across the fields, and Joyce and her partner, Felix Cosme, spend a major proportion of each day in the kennels cleaning and mending them, plus time spent socialising and training the dogs, so that there is never a shortage of human company.

There are two whelping rooms, equipped with heat-lamps and whelping boxes. When the puppies are old enough to leave their mother they are taken into another kennel, which has a puppy run for use in warm weather. There is a separate grooming room, which is most important

The Beagold kennels.

for dogs with long coats, and even dogs with smooth coats like to be brushed and attended to on a regular basis. In the dog kitchen there is a deep-freeze cabinet and a fridge for the meat. The dry all-in-one food and dog biscuits are stored in large plastic barrels. The feeding bowls are stored in cupboards, and steel bowls are preferred, as they are easier to clean. The Beagold kennels cater for a number of different breeds, so each dish is individually labelled – it would not do for the small Swedish Vallhund to be given the rations intended for the Bouvier des Flandres! Some Beardies and Border Collies put on weight very quickly, and others need more food to keep up their weight, and so the rations for each dog are weighed at every feed.

The dogs that live this sort of life in kennels, not knowing anything different, are fit and healthy. They exercise when they want to and rest when they feel tired, usually finding a favourite spot in the sunshine. The kennel routine is designed to keep them interested and happy, and by feeding at the same time every day feeding problems are avoided. The dogs enjoy their daily exercise and look forward to their show days. They are transported to shows in a wire cage, in the car, and when the blanket is put down in the cage, they settle down with no trouble, even on the longest journey.

Pat is a firm believer in kennelling all her dogs, and she has designed a set-up to suit all breeds at her Wellknowe kennels. The adult dogs are kennelled singly, as this ensures that each dog receives its correct food and additives, and it is also the best way to see exactly what each dog is, or is not, eating. It also enables each animal to have the food and conditions that suit it the best. The kennels are open-fronted to allow direct access to fresh air, both in the summer and winter. However, great care is taken to prevent draughts, direct wind-paths and rain from blowing into the kennel. The dogs can all see each other, which prevents them feeling isolated. Pat believes

The type of kennel used and prefered at Wellknowe.

that total relaxation can only be achieved by a home-life designed on a personal basis, and so individual tastes are always catered for at the Wellknowe kennels. Each kennel has its own sleeping area and its own 6 foot by 12 foot covered run. Some dogs like sleeping benches, some prefer boxes or beds, and others prefer jumping up on to a shelf-type bench. The floors of the runs are always made with paving stones or local slate, as this is better for the dogs than concrete, which has a tendency to hold damp. A small area has a sawdust covering, in case of accidents. The beds or benches are covered in carpet, wool blankets or special bedding material. This is secured to the sleeping area, where it hopefully stays intact. This is the dog's own home, but they spend most of the daylight hours (weather permitting) in a one-acre paddock. Group exercising is much favoured because of the play element, and the total freedom afforded in natural surroundings. For the current show dogs, large concrete runs take the place of grass paddocks, and, once again, group exercising is preferable. These dogs are also road-walked, or more truthfully, bicycle-walked, to ensure good muscle tone and tight feet.

However, the larger percentage of Bearded Collies bought for show and as pets are kept in the house and live a life of ease and luxury. If the number of dogs increases they may have to take their turn in a kennel, but with just a couple of dogs, both can live perfectly happily in the house. The Bearded Collie invariably adapts well to home-life, and enjoys being one of the family. Owners should restrict the amount of space they give to a new puppy at first. The area allocated to the puppy can be wired off, or a little gate can be erected. At night the pup can have its own bench or bed, with water and newspaper put down on the floor to soak up any urine, and to make it easy to pick up any mess, because the puppy will need to toilet at night until it is older. There is absolutely no need to come down in the morning and find the whole kitchen or utility room dotted with mess and urine. If the puppy has its space restricted right at the beginning it will learn where it sleeps and spends its nights, and it will adjust to the restriction very quickly. A puppy that is allowed the freedom to sleep wherever it wants will take that much longer before it learns where it can mess. If it has its own little haven right from the start, it will be quite happy at night, and when the owners go out it will settle down and wait for their return without resorting to destructive behaviour. Chew toys are useful for keeping a puppy amused when it is on its own.

A puppy that is allowed the run of the house will resent suddenly being restricted to a limited space. However, this is invariably what happens when it has chewed the carpet, messed in the other rooms, and had a go at the furniture. The irate owner will then do what should have been done in the first place, and restrict the puppy to its own little corner and bed. The problem is never so acute in the summer when the pup can spend a lot more time in the garden or yard, and that is where the puppy will mess, and will even cry to be let out to its favourite spot. Bearded Collies, like all puppies, can be destructive, and the tell-tale signs of chewed wallpaper and woodwork in bathrooms, bedroom and stairs indicate a puppy that has not been kept under proper control. Joyce once sold a puppy to a very houseproud lady, who gave assurances that she would be sensible, and she would only allow the pup to live downstairs in a large washroom with access to the garden. However, she phoned a month later to ask if she could return the puppy as it was chewing the stair carpet and the landing stairs. So much for her promise to keep the puppy downstairs!

New owners should understand that the Bearded Collie puppy is a breed in the Working Group, and arrangements should be made for its comfort – but in sensible surroundings. The Beardie's ancestors were drover's dogs, and they lived and worked on a farm, thriving on a healthy and active outdoor life. They slept in barns and outside sheds, and only if they were very lucky were they allowed in the farmhouse kitchen, and this was only when they had been trained and knew how to behave. When we, as breeders, bring these dogs into our homes and expect them to be thoroughly domesticated and accept this completely different life, we do them an injustice, unless we give them sensible training and understanding. The Bearded Collie's intelligence should never be left to stagnate; it should always be given some interest in life. They are good at Obedience: many owners have taken their dogs to compete on the Working Tests, and the training needed for the show ring keeps them active and happy.

Chapter Six

THE VERSATILE BEARDIE

The Bothkennar Bearded Collies, which formed the foundation of the breed, typify all the essential ingredients in today's Breed Standard. They show the sensible broad head, a good arch of neck, lovely well-laid shoulders, good depth of brisket, correct length of body, well-angled hindquarters and low hocks. The true, sensible, working Beardie did not have the frills and fancies of many of today's show Beardies. The breed was referred to as the Highland Collie, and it was a strong agile animal, whose strengths lay in its capacity and stamina to work all day in all weathers. To do the job that it was bred for, it needed to conserve energy and stamina. It needed a sensible outlook on life, and brains to match. It needed well-laid shoulders to enable the dog to stop and start, to turn quickly at any speed over any terrain. The lay of the shoulders was also essential in providing sufficient forward reach to make the dog's stride economical and energy-saving. It needed the depth of brisket to give plenty of heart and lung room, the length of body to complement both ends, the daylight under him, the well-angled stifles and low hocks that allowed it to move forward with an economical stride, as high hocks would make this impossible. The croup correctly angled, leading to the low-set tail, assisted the dog when slowing its speed, and the harsh, weatherproof coat stopped it becoming soaked to the skin and chilled during long wet days and nights at its work. This was the working Bearded Collie, the dog that looked after and controlled the stock. If this animal had constructional faults it could not have worked, as the very nature of its construction is the key to its ability to endure stress and strain, and to work tirelessly in all weathers. In other words, it must be sound in every department. An animal who was unsound would have had no place as a worker on a farm. If it could not jump a stone wall or gate cleanly, and turn on landing, or gallop up a fell-side, twisting and turning as it went, or if it could not do twenty miles at one go, on hard roads and remain sound and ready to do its job the next day, it would have been discarded. There is no

Quinbury Stormdrifter At Runival CD.Ex, a qualified mountain rescue dog, who won Best of Breed at Crufts

One of the working Wellknowe Beardies. Note that the dog's body is well covered with harsh, weather resistant hair, but it is not so long as to hinder work.

sentimentality in choosing working dogs – they have to have everything right, they must be workmanlike, and most importantly, they must have a sensible, calm outlook and a functional brain.

However, the Bearded Collie was rejected in favour of smaller working breeds, and its future was very bleak. On the plus-side, the breed was a sound, brave companion, free of restricting defects, and its appeal was apparent to its small band of supporters. Today the Bearded Collie flourishes in great numbers, and is loved and enjoyed by many. There are Beardies all around the world that still work stock, and indeed in some areas the working side is encouraged. They can still be found working in Scotland, and still compare favourably with their ancestors. The breed today fulfils many other roles: pet-dog, show dog, guide dog for the blind, or agility dog – or any combination of some or all of these roles. The Beardie's naturally happy, outgoing temperament endears it to many people, and in the main, it gives happiness and pleasure to many people the world over, and receives it, too.

Denise Barley and her Bearded Collie devoted much of their time to rescuing people in trouble at Aviemore, in the Scottish Highlands, where the snow, ice, and freezing conditions would frighten all but the most stout-hearted. An article was published in the National Press, featuring 'Bob', complete with 'tubegrip', to stop the coat on his legs, feet and head from 'balling' up. He later won Best of Breed at Crufts – no mean feat. He is a son of Ch. Potterdale Patch Of Blue. Denise worked several of her dogs in the snow, but now prefers to show and do Obedience and Working Trials. In fact 'Bob', or Quinbury Stormdrifter at Runival, is qualified CD.Ex. His father, Ch. Potterdale Patch Of Blue, was retired to a farm home, where he showed an aptitude for farm work. In fact, there are many Beardies that still work on the farm for their living. Douglas Dawson, who lives in Scotland, is a sales representative and travels to many farms in the course of his work. He sees the Bearded Collie as they were shown in the old prints, shorter in coat, and more workmanlike. Nick Broadbridge (Sallen) and Tom Muirhead both breed for the the working side and supply many farmers in Scotland. Tom Muirhead works his dogs on the farm all year round. There are some Beardies working in Cumbria; one farm in particular, at Bassenthwaite, regularly uses Bearded Collies for work. Pat has supplied several Beardies to other farms, both in Cumbria and other areas.

On the Obedience trail, pride of place in the UK must go to the only Bearded Collie Obedience Champion, Scapa, owned by Jenni Wiggins, formerly Cooke; her name became part of Jenni's prefix Scapafield. She was a superb worker. Jenni then trained Ch. Osmart Black Lorraine to Test C standard, and won at that level. She would have liked her to be a second Obedience Champion like Scapa, who stood supreme – and is likely to do so for the foreseeable future, as few Beardie owners achieve such a high standard. Ch. Bosky Glen Of Bothkennar, the father of Scapa, competed in Obedience, winning up to Test B and C, handled by Barbara Iremonger. Ob. Ch. Scapa had a versatile brother called Tannochbrae, owned by Miss Morriss. A third littermate, Ch. Beagold Ella, owned by Joyce, became a star in the show ring. As Joyce's second Beardie, she filled a major role in the Beagold kennel as a good brood bitch.

To date, there are five Champions that have passed the Senior Working Test. They are: the first to qualify, Ch. Heathermead Handsome, owned by Lyn Evans and bred by Michelle James; Ch. Holtend Chiff Chaff, owned and bred by Dr Margaret Buckley; Ch. Gillaber Highland Lament, owned and bred by the Gill and Cooke partnership; Ch. Deedledee Carefree Rupert, owned and bred by Mrs Wendy Rawson; and Ch. Beardievale Village Gossip, owned by Tricia Poole and bred by Burgoine. Bond Of Bothkennar won a Senior Working Trials Certificate in those far-off days when there were only Senior and Junior Trials. Quinbury Wellington Boot, owned by Miss Sarjeant was the first Beardie to qualify as Tracker Dog (TD) at Working Trials. Pat's Ch. Charncroft Cavalcade was the only Champion to be a full-time working dog at the same time as gaining his title. He was the foundation of the Wellknowe kennel; his ancestors were from Bothkennar breeding, and Pat believed that he typified her interpretation of the Breed Standard.

The Bearded Collie is an ideal breed to be taught both Obedience and Agility. Several have excelled in these activities, in the UK and abroad. When Beagold Black Tiffany was sent to Mr and Mrs Blumiere in America, they must have wondered about the breeding of the bitch, as she was not at all like the glamorous grey and white, or brown and white dogs and bitches that had been exported to the United States. Tiffany was a descendant of Tuftine Brigadier, and she inherited his coat and his colour, and as she matured the Blumieres realised that she had also inherited his brains. In fact, Tiffany was the only one in the litter that inherited so many of Tuftine Brigadier's characteristics and working capabilities. Recognising her potential, Joan Blumiere started training her right from the beginning, and not only did this bitch excel in the show ring by winning her American and Canadian Championships, she also added the titles Utility Dog, Sch. Ad. TT. Register of Merit. Tiffany received the Best Lifetime Achievement Award, but sadly it was awarded posthumously. There are many of her descendants achieving high honours in the Show and Obedience rings in the USA, but it will be a hard task to beat that beautiful black and white Beardie called Tiffany. Tiffany's grand-dam, Wishanger Bridge Of Gairn, was taken to compete in the Working Tests and would have done extremely well if her owner had persevered, but she only passed the Primary Test and went no further, as she spent

Mrs Jenni Wiggins' Ob. Ch. Scapa in action at Obedience trials.

'Dieter' (Ch. Sunbrees Sorcerer – Sunbrees Serenade) qualified as a Guide Dog.

In the years to come...

you'll be glad you had...

Scotchgard™ protector.

Beardies have frequently been used in advertising campaigns.

Reproduced with kind permission of 3M United kingdom PLC.

more of her time in the beauty show ring. The Beardie has adapted well to Agility competitions, and Mrs Wendy Rawson's Ch. Deedledee Care Free Rupert and his father, Ian Copus's Int. Ch. Rallentando Rookie, are both successful in this field. Rupert was also a CC winner at Crufts. Many Beardies enjoy Agility and it does fulfil a need for such an active breed. For many years Pat had a demonstration team, which latterly included two Beardies. One was taught hoop-jumping and hurdling, at which he excelled as he was a natural athlete. The second dog was a great retriever, and graduated to retrieving a 'flaming' dumb-bell, alight at both ends. This he did with great gusto, but Pat used to put a type of bonnet on him before this trick, or a lot of his head coat would be singed. He went on to a 'flaming hoop', but she had to discontinue this because of the same problem of singed hair.

Many Beardies work as Therapy or 'PAT' dogs, another role of invaluable help to the sick and infirm, and the Beardie's wonderful temperament and friendly disposition make it ideal for this type of work. Mrs Margaret Harkin's Rallentando Rula, pet name 'Charity', is a registered PAT dog. Margaret takes her to visit the local hospital fairly regularly, knowing that she will cheer up the patients. Charity knows her business and is always on her best behaviour, first meeting and charming the nurses, before she is taken to the wards. She greets each elderly person like a long lost friend, and is usually rewarded with a titbit, as her visit is the highlight of the day. Some of the patients have had dogs in the past, and they miss their pets terribly. For the very sick and withdrawn patients, the visit gives them a reason to talk and come out of themselves when they can stroke the lovely coat of a Bearded Collie.

Several Beardies have qualified or passed out as Guide Dogs for the Blind. The first to do so were a dog and bitch bred by Betty Foster (Bredon). Ten years ago Barbara Iremonger (Sunbrees) gave two six-week-old puppies to be trained. The Association wanted two bitches, but Barbara believed that the males were better suited to the role of guide dog. She eventually let them have one female – who did not make the grade – and the dog, Dieter, who was an excellent guide dog. He had his coat cut short to avoid too much grooming for his blind owner. He was by Ch. Sunbrees Sorcerer out of Sunbrees Serenade.

The Bearded Collie's attractive appearance and intelligent disposition have made it an ideal breed to choose in the world of advertising and show business. Jeannie Of Bothkennar was the first film star, appearing in *Day of Grace*. Ch. Potterdale Classic Of Moonhill (Cassie), Best in Show at Crufts in 1989 earned respect as a fine ambassador of the breed, whenever she was filmed. Int. Ch. Bobby Of Bothkennar was a stand-in in a South African film, as a 'mother'. The real mum had stage fright, but Bobby lay down, had his underparts smeared with minced meat, and hey presto, he became a mother, not objecting to the hungry puppies at all! Teddy Brown At Beagold was taken to a studio to be photographed for Christmas cards and had to sit with an elderly man by a roaring fire. The fire had to be blazing for the red-coloured flames to set a cosy scene. Poor Teddy could hardly bear the heat, and neither could the ornaments on the Christmas Tree. The heat was so intense they started to melt, and had to be replaced in double-quick time. Advertising agents find the Bearded Collie an ideal subject; the Beardie pups look like pretty little pandas, with their fluffy faces and low-set ears – their expression is so soft and appealing that they have been featured on cards, jigsaw puzzles and posters. The adult Bearded Collie is very easy to train, and even if they have never been in front of a camera before, they behave like film stars and pose professionally. Mick and Irene Kiff have taken their Beardies several times to be filmed for an advertising campaign for Scotchguard Protector, featuring muddy Beardie and pups on a carpet.

When the Bearded Collie was first shown we had to suffer those people who came to the show just to criticise and give their opinion on the unsuitability of Bearded Collies in the show ring, when they should be on the farm working or out in the fields in their natural environment. However, the dogs adjusted very well to the show ring – this was just one more facet of their versatility. Owners who cared about their dogs did not want them to lose their intelligence, and so in Britain a Working Test was devised in 1969. The Bearded Collie Club and the Southern Bearded Collie Club worked together to organise these tests, and the other clubs soon followed. This was a pattern that has been followed in the USA and elsewhere, as no one wanted the Bearded Collie to degenerate into a glamorous show dog that had no encouragement to use its brain. Finally, credit must go the Bearded Collie in its role as a family pet. The breed is intelligent and friendly, and is loyal to its human pack members. There is a delightful story which illustrates this, dating back to 1930, before the breed was officially recognised. In fact, the

The Duke Of Gloucester presents 'Prince' with the Gugnuc Collar for his bravery in saving ten-year-old Hilda Bright from drowning.

family in question thought 'Prince' was an Old English Sheepdog with a tail. Apparently, ten-year-old Hilda Bright fell into a pond when she was climbing over the railings to pick catkins. Hilda was wearing a mackintosh and Wellington boots, and would certainly have drowned had it not been for Prince. He leapt into the water and let Hilda grab on to his coat, and then barked loudly until help arrived. His bravery was recognised when he was awarded the *Daily Mirror* Gugnuc Collar, which was presented to Hilda and the dog by the Duke of Gloucester at Crufts in 1930.

Chapter Seven

THE BREED STANDARD

The Bearded Collie has travelled a very varied path since its first recordings as a rough working dog to the glamorous breed that is so popular in the show ring today. In *Dogs of Scotland,* written in the early 1800s, the Beardie is described as "A big rough 'tousy' looking tyke with a coat not unlike a doormat, the texture of the hair hard and fibry, and the ears hanging close to the head". In Cassell's *New Book of the Dog*, the Beardie is called the Scottish Beardie or Highland Collie, and is described as "of heavy build, powerful limbs, thick, short neck, heavy shoulders and thick skin. There is a rugged grandeur about him that resembles the Scottish Deerhound and Otter Hound. The colour is varied, cream-coloured specimens are not uncommon, and snow-white with orange or black markings may often be seen, but the popular colour is grizzly-grey."

The first official Breed Standard for the Bearded Collie was drawn up in 1912 (Bearded Collie Society, Edinburgh), but few shepherds registered their dogs with either the Kennel Club or with the International Sheepdog Society, until Mrs Willison registered her first Beardie in 1949. She laid the foundation of Bearded Collie bloodlines in Britain and overseas, and she described the Bothkenner Beardies as:

GENERAL APPEARANCE: An active dog with none of the stumpiness of the Bobtail and which, though strongly made, does not look too heavy; the face should have a sharp enquiring expression. Movement should be free and active.

HEAD AND SKULL: Large and square, plenty of space for the brain. Nose large and square and black, except with brown or fawn coats when brown is permitted.

EYES: To tone with coat in colour; wall eye, either single or double, permitted with merle coat.

The eyes should be set rather widely apart, big, soft and affectionate, but not protruding. Eyebrows slightly elevated, covered with shaggy hair.

EARS: Medium size, drooping, covered with shaggy hair.

MOUTH: Teeth large and white, never overshot or undershot.

NECK: Must be of fair length, muscular and slightly arched.

FOREQUARTERS: Legs straight with good bone, pasterns flexible without weakness, covered with shaggy hair right down to the feet.

BODY: Fairly long, back level with well sprung ribs and strong loins, chest deep, shoulders flat, straight front.

HINDQUARTERS: Legs muscular at thighs with well-bent stifles and hocks.

FEET: Oval in shape, soles well padded, toes arched and close together.

COAT: Must be double, the under one soft, furry and close, the outer one hard, strong and shaggy. The legs covered all round, little hair on the nose affording contrast to the shaggy 'beard' running from each side.

COLOUR: Immaterial, but preference given to slate or reddish fawn, with or without white collie marking.

SIZE: Dogs 20ins to 24ins at the shoulder.
    Bitches from 18ins.

FAULTS: Thick round ribs, too rotund in body, too short in length, meagre short tail, narrow skull, bare legs, too long or too short nose.

The English Kennel Club revised all its Breed Standards in 1986, and, although the version that is used today is a fair description, it lacks the detail which can bring so much to the understanding of a breed.

THE ENGLISH BREED STANDARD

GENERAL APPEARANCE Lean active dog, longer than it is high in approximate proportion of 5 to 4, measured from point of chest to point of buttock. Bitches may be slightly longer. Though strongly made, should show plenty of daylight under the body and should not look too heavy. Bright enquiring expression is a distinctive feature.

CHARACTERISTICS: Alert, lively, self-confident and active.

TEMPERAMENT: Steady, intelligent working dog, with no signs of nervousness or aggression.

HEAD AND SKULL: Head in proportion to size. Skull broad, flat and square, distance between stop and occiput being equal to width between orifices of ears. Muzzle strong in equal length to distance between stop and occiput. Whole effect being that of a dog with strength of muzzle and plenty of brain room. Moderate stop. Nose large and square, generally black but normally following coat colour in blues and browns. Nose and lips of solid colour, without spots or patches. Pigmentation of lips and eye rims follows nose colour.

EYES: Toning with coat colour, set widely apart and large, soft and affectionate, not protruding. Eyebrows arched up and forward but not so long as to obscure eyes.

EARS: Of medium size drooping. When alert, ears lift at base, level with, but not above top of skull, increasing apparent breadth of skull.

MOUTH: Teeth large and white. Jaws strong with a perfect, regular and complete scissor bite preferred i.e. upper teeth closely overlapping lower teeth and set square to the jaws. Level bite tolerated but undesirable.

NECK: Moderate length, muscular and slightly arched.

FOREQUARTERS. Shoulders sloping well back. Legs straight and vertical with good bone, covered with shaggy hair all round. Pasterns flexible without weakness.

BODY: Length of back comes from length of ribcage and not that of loin. Back level and ribs well sprung but not barrelled. Loin strong and chest deep, giving plenty of heart and lung room.

HINDQUARTERS: Well muscled with good second thighs, well bent stifles and low hocks. Lower leg falls at right angles to ground and, in normal stance, is just behind a line vertically below point of buttocks.

FEET: Oval in shape with soles well padded. Toes arched and close together, well covered with hair, including between pads.

TAIL: Set low, without kink or twist, and long enough for end of bone to reach at least point of hock. Carried low with an upward swirl at tip whilst standing or walking, may be extended at speed. Never carried over back. Covered with abundant hair.

COAT: Double with soft, furry and close undercoat. Outercoat flat, harsh, strong and shaggy, free from woolliness and curl, though slight wave permissible. Length and density of hair sufficient to provide a protective coat and to enhance shape of dog, but not enough to obscure natural lines of body. Coat must not be trimmed in any way. Bridge of nose sparsely covered with hair slightly longer on side just to cover lips. From cheeks, lower lips and under the chin, coat increases in length towards chest, forming typical beard.

GAIT: Movement supple, smooth and long reaching, covering ground with the minimum of effort.

COLOUR: Slate grey, reddish fawn, black, blue, all shades of grey, brown and sandy with or without white markings. When white occurs, it appears on foreface, as a blaze on skull, on tip of tail, on chest, legs and feet, and if round the collar, roots of white hair should not extend behind shoulder. White should not appear above hocks on outside of hind legs. Slight tan markings are acceptable on eyebrows, inside ears, on cheeks, under top of tail and on legs where white joins main colour.

SIZE: Ideal height : Dogs 53 - 56 cms (21 - 22ins); Bitches 51 - 53 cms (20 - 21ins). Overall quality and proportions should be considered before size but excessive variations from the ideal height should be discouraged.

FAULTS: Any departure from the foregoing points should be considered a fault and the seriousness with which the fault should be regarded should be in exact proportion to its degree.

NOTE: Male animals should have two apparently normal testicles fully descended into the scrotum.

Reproduced by kind permission of the English Kennel Club.

In America, the Breed Standard published in 1978 is currently in use. In many ways this is an excellent Standard, but it is important that breeders and exhibitors take note of exactly what is required.

THE AMERICAN BREED STANDARD

CHARACTERISTICS: The Bearded Collie is hardy and active, with an aura of strength and agility characteristic of a real working dog. Bred for centuries as a companion and servant of man, the Bearded Collie is a devoted and intelligent member of the family. He is stable and self confident, showing no signs of shyness or aggression. This is a natural and unspoiled breed.

GENERAL APPEARANCE: The Bearded Collie is a medium sized shaggy dog with a medium length coat that follows the natural lines of the body and allows plenty of daylight under the body. The body is long and lean, and though strongly made does not appear heavy. A bright inquiring expression is a distinctive feature of the breed. The Bearded Collie should be shown in a natural stance.

HEAD: The head is in proportion to the size of the dog. The skull is broad and flat, the stop is moderate, the cheeks are well filled in beneath the eyes, the muzzle is strong and full, the foreface is equal in length to the distance between the stop and occiput. The nose is large and squarish. A snipey muzzle is to be penalised.

EYES: The eyes are large, expressive, soft and affectionate, but not round nor protruding, and are set widely apart. The eyebrows are arched to the sides to frame the eyes and are long enough to blend smoothly into the coat on the sides of the head.

EARS: The ears are medium sized, hanging and covered with long hair. They are set level with the eyes. When the dog is alert the ears have a slight lift at the base.

TEETH: The teeth are strong and white, meeting in a scissor bite. Full dentition is desirable.

NECK: The neck should be in proportion to the length of the body, strong and slightly arched, blending smoothly into the shoulders.

FOREQUARTERS: The shoulders are well laid back at an angle of approximately forty five degrees; a line drawn from the highest point of the shoulder to the forward point of articulation approximates a right angle with a line from the forward point of articulation to the point of the elbow. The top of the shoulder blades lie in against the withers, but they slope outwards from there sufficiently to accommodate the desired spring of ribs. The legs are straight and vertical with substantial but not heavy bone and are covered with shaggy hair all around. The pasterns are flexible without weakness.

BODY: The body is longer than it is high in approximate ratio of five to four, length measured from point of chest to point of buttocks, height measured at the highest point of the withers. The length of back comes from the length of ribcage and not that of loin. The back is level. The ribs are well sprung from the spine but flat at the sides. The chest is deep, reaching at least to the elbows. The loins are strong. The level back blends smoothly into the curve of the rump. A flat croup or a steep croup is to be severely penalised.

HINDQUARTERS: The hind legs are powerful and muscular at the thighs with well bent stifles. The hocks are low. In normal stance the bones below the hocks are perpendicular to the ground and parallel to each other when viewed from the rear, the hind feet fall just behind a perpendicular line from the point of buttocks, when viewed from the side. The legs are covered with shaggy hair all round.

TAIL: The tail is set low and is long enough for the end bone to reach at least the point of the hocks. It is normally carried low with an upward swirl at the tip while the dog is standing. When the dog is excited or in motion, the curve is accentuated and the tail may be raised but it never carried beyond a vertical line. The tail is covered with abundant hair.

FEET: The feet are oval in shape with the soles well padded. The toes are arched and close together and well covered with hair including between the pads.

COAT: The coat is double with the undercoat soft, furry and close. The outercoat is flat, harsh, strong and shaggy, free from wooliness and curl, although a slight wave is permissible. The coat falls naturally to either side but must not be artificially parted. The length and density of the hair are sufficient to provide a protective coat and to enhance the shape of the dog, but not so profuse as to obscure the natural lines of the body. The dog should be shown naturally as is consistent with good grooming, but the coat must not be trimmed in any way. On the head, the bridge of the nose is sparsely covered with hair which is slightly longer on the sides to cover the lips. From the cheeks the lower lips and under the chin, the coat increases in length towards the chest, forming a typical beard. An excessively long silky coat or one which has been trimmed in any way, must be severely penalised.

COLOR – COAT: All Bearded Collies are born either black, blue, brown or fawn, with or without white markings. With maturity the color may lighten so that a born black may become any shade of grey, from black to slate to silver; a born brown from chocolate to sandy; blues and fawns also show shades from light to dark. Where white occurs, it only appears on the fore face as a blaze, on the skull, on the tip of the tail, on the chest, legs and feet and around the neck. The white hair does not grow on the body, behind the shoulder, nor on the face to surround the eyes. Tan markings occasionally appear and are acceptable on the eyebrows, inside the ears, on the cheeks, under the root of the tail and on the legs where white joins the main color.

PIGMENTATION: Pigmentation on the Bearded Collie follows the coat color. In a born black the eye rim, nose and lips are black, whereas in the born blue the pigmentation is a blue grey color. A born brown dog has brown pigmentation and born fawn a correspondingly lighter brown. The pigmentation is completely filled in and shows no sign of spots.

EYES: Eye color will generally tone with coat color. In a born blue or fawn, the distinctively lighter eyes are correct and must not be penalised.

SIZE: The ideal height at the withers is 21-22 inches for adult dogs and 20-21 inches for adult bitches. Height over and under the ideal is a disqualification. The express objects of this criterion is to insure that the Bearded Collie remains a medium sized dog.

GAIT: Movement is free, supple and powerful. Balance combines good reach in forequarters with strong drive in hindquarters. The back remains firm and level. The feet are lifted only enough to clear the ground giving the impression that the dog glides along, making minimum contact. Movement is lithe and flexible to enable the dog to make the sharp turns and sudden stops required of the sheep dog. When viewed from the front or

rear, the front and rear legs travel in the same plane from shoulder and hip joint to pads at all speeds. Legs remain straight, but feet move inward as speed increases with the edges of the feet converging on a center line at a fast trot.

SERIOUS FAULTS: Snipey muzzle. Flat croup or steep croup. Excessively long silky coat. Trimmed or sculptured coat. Height over or under the ideal.

Reproduced by kind permission of the American Kennel Club.

ANALYSIS OF THE BREED STANDARD

The ability to work is natural to many breeds, in spite of man's interference, but to keep the animal looking and behaving as the Breed Standard intended it to be, appears to have escaped many newcomers to the breed. Obviously, everyone has their own interpretation, but sadly, there are some breeders and exhibitors who have never read or studied what has been written in the Standard. Invariably, these are the people who question why they have not been placed in the winning line-up and who argue when a glaring fault is pointed out. Today there is an increased awareness of the need to educate newcomers to the breed, and lectures and seminars are arranged on a regular basis by the various breed clubs. Hopefully this will pay dividends in the long term and future generations will still see the beautiful, lithe intelligent Bearded Collie 'as God made him'.

However, it is important for exhibitors to realise that every judge has their own personal interpretation of the Breed Standard. Some judges may overlook a fault because they do not think it spoils the overall picture, but another judge may penalise that same fault severely. For instance, when Joyce is judging she is prepared to forgive one or two teeth missing; her argument is that this would not stop the dog from working. She would also place a Beardie with a less than flowing coat – in fact she prefers the Beardie with a body-hugging coat of the correct texture. She considers a slight loss of pigment around the mouth to be a minor fault, but she will not accept loss of pigment on the nose or around the eyes. The Beardie is a natural, lively breed, and she likes to see animation in a dog she is judging. This liveliness may result in the dog's tail rising higher than the back, and she will accept this, so long as it is not curled over the back. If the animation develops into an activity such as barking or jumping up when there is clapping, she will not penalise the dog. Pat, however, is opposed to such behaviour as she believes this indicates an excitable temperament which is not suited to a working dog. Both viewpoints have equal relevance, and both accord with the Breed Standard. If all judges saw things the same way, they would always come up with the same winner. This is the essence of competing in the show ring, and it is why all those involved find it such a fascinating occupation.

The Breed Standard must always be regarded as the cornerstone of the breed, and each heading that is listed should be considered in detail.

GENERAL APPEARANCE

The requirement in the English Standard of a "Lean active dog, longer than it is high in approximate proportion of 5 to 4 measured from point of chest to point of buttock", should be

The Bearded Collie has a completely different outline to the Old English Sheepdog.

The Beardie...

The Old English Sheepdog.....

adhered to rigidly. In the American Standard "an approximate ratio of five to four" is mentioned under the heading for 'Body', but in the section on 'General Appearance' the description is confined to "the body is long and lean", which could mean, in practice, the body being of any length, which usually results in a drop behind the withers and a weak back. Bitches may be slightly longer, according to the English Standard, but a cautionary note should be added. The whole appearance of the bitch is foreign when there is a parting from nose to tail on an endless length of body. This cosmetic alteration is sad for the breed, and is usually accompanied by trimming of the feet, and sculpturing of the facial hair. The gorgeous, natural presentation is a

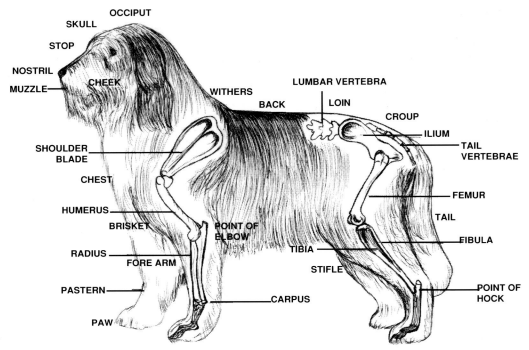

Anatomy of the Bearded Collie.

feature of the breed, which is in the Working Group, and does not need to be glamorised like a Toy or Utility Group breed.The American Standard states that the Bearded Collie should be shown in a "natural stance", which is a very important point. This is a working breed and there should be no need for the handler to go down on hands and knees to prop up the dog's head and support its body.

It is a shame that the wording "and none of the stumpiness of the Bobtail" has been lost from present Breed Standards, as this helped to give the impression of a more lithe and active dog than the larger, cumbersome Old English Sheepdog.

CHARACTERISTICS

It is obvious from reading the description in the American Standard that this harks back to the dog's working past, and the Bearded Collie in the show ring in America and in Great Britain is not the same unspoilt breed of former years. The result of breeders aiming for long, flowing coats is that the texture is now soft, and certainly not weather-resistant. Later the Standard suggests that the coat be "harsh", yet the number of Beardies, both in the Britain and overseas, that have the correct texture and length of coat is very few.

TEMPERAMENT

There was a situation just a little while ago, when Beardie breeders could not believe that temperament was starting to deteriorate. One or two dogs especially became aggressive in the show ring. Thank goodness this aggressiveness seems to have disappeared. We still have very lively, and active dogs, although some bitches can be noisy and annoying. Endlesss barking, for no good reason, should be discouraged immediately.

A typical Bearded Collie should be:
ALERT: Aware of everything that is going on, with an enquiring expression.
ACTIVE: Full of life, moving with a smooth, ground-covering, lively gait.
STEADY: Should be trained, when the need arises, to accept responsible behaviour.
INTERESTED IN SURROUNDINGS: A dead-pan expression is untypical of the breed.
FRIENDLY AND BIDDABLE: Allowed to show friendliness by wagging tail, but not jumping up.
THE GUARDING INSTINCT: Should only be allowed to surface when the need arises.

An untypical Bearded Collie is:
WILD: Uncontrolled behaviour, jumping up.
AGGRESSIVE: This should be stopped immediately, especially before the puppy reaches adulthood.
SHY AND NERVOUS: Backing away from the judge; the reason for this should be found out before the dog is taken to another show.
LETHARGIC: When the owner props up the dog when trying to pose it in the show ring, it begins to rely on support.
THE HEAVY PLODDING LETHARGIC MOVEMENT: Consult the veterinary surgeon.
SEDATED: Travel sickness tablets do not always have the desired effect. The sign that tranquilliser tablets have been used is when the dog's third eyelid covers the eye.

HEAD AND SKULL

The head is the first part of the dog that the judge sees, and it is obviously a very important feature of the breed. The skull must be felt to see that it is broad, flat and square. Joyce always feels to make sure that there is a good stop and the correct length of muzzle.

EYES

Eye colour should tone with coat colour, as stated in the Standard, and this means that the blue Bearded Collie has dove-grey blue eyes; brown eyes are incorrect. The American Standard does not cover this point. Brown or very dark eyes are correct in the born black; they can be a shade lighter if the dog changes to slate grey or light grey as it becomes an adult. The born fawn has light fawn eyes. The born brown should also have eye colour to match the coat, so if the coat is dark brown it should have dark brown eyes, and if the coat is very pale, the eyes can be paler. Wall eyes or split wall eyes as in merle-coloured dogs are not acceptable in the Beardie breed. Yellow eyes look hard and foreign to the breed, even in dogs that have the palest brown coat.

The head should form a blunt wedge, when viewed from the front.

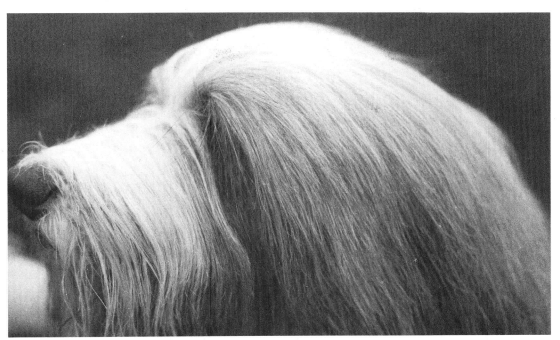

Blunt wedge when viewed from the side.

A balanced head, well groomed, with no artificial plucking around the eyes.

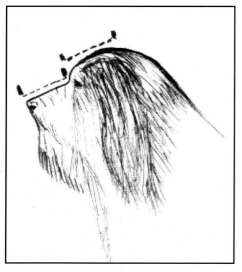

Balanced head, showing correct proportions and good stop.

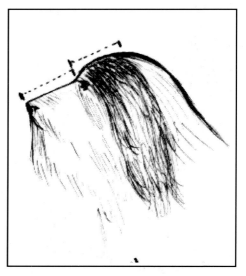

Longer in muzzle than length of skull, not enough stop.

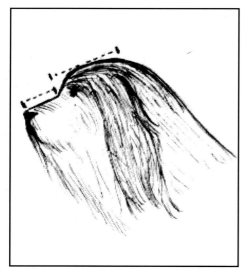

Too short in muzzle.

No stop.

Excellent ear-set, flat skull and good texture coat.

EARS

A narrow skull usually means that the Beardie will have high-set ears, although the Standard asks for "medium-sized and drooping ears". The best expression seems to be found in puppies that are born with large drooping ears. They stay low-set, and eventually become well furnished and held correctly, flat to the skull. It would help breeders if it was added to the Standard that the ears should lie flat against the skull. On the Continent the judges penalise the Beardie with a fold in the ears. High-set ears should be penalised as they alter the expression of the Beardie.

MOUTH

"Scissor bite preferred" can be interpreted as "a level bite will be accepted". When the dog has a level bite the teeth will soon wear down. There has been some evidence recently of Beardies that have problems shutting their mouths, as the teeth in the rear are not correctly placed. This could be caused by puppies having their first teeth misplaced, so that they go up into the gums of the top jaw. It is believed to be an inherited problem.

NECK

The beautiful arch of the neck should be a major feature of the breed. Short stuffy necks look as if the dog is unbalanced.

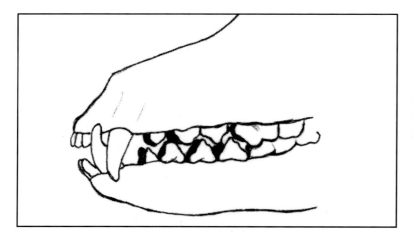

Correct scissor bite: the top teeth fit into the bottom set.

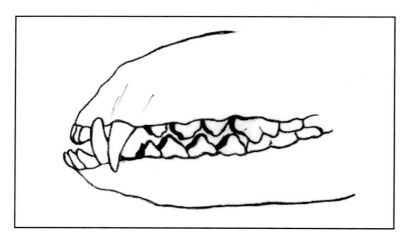

Undershot mouth.

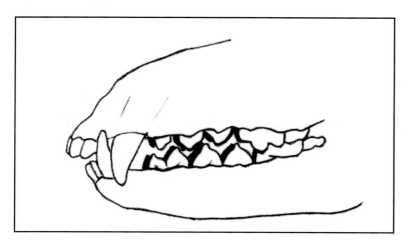

Overshot mouth.

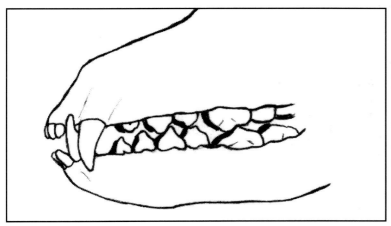

An inherited fault when the mouth will not close as the teeth at the back of the jaw are incorrectly placed.

FOREQUARTERS

It would be hard to improve on the wording of the sections that cover 'Forequarters', 'Body' and 'Hindquarters' in the American Standard, and the English Standard certainly suffers in comparison.

The shoulders should form a 90 per cent angle, with the shoulder blade at the withers only separated by the vertebrae, but it must slope outwards from there sufficiently to accommodate the desired spring of rib. With the profuse coat on a Bearded Collie it is important that a judge does not just play piano on the topline but feels under the coat, especially for angle of shoulder, and legs straight and vertical, with no 'ten to two' or 'quarter to three' placing of the feet.

BODY

The length of the body should come from the length of rib and ribcage, and not from the loin. When Pat is judging she likes to feel for the width of chest with her hand cupped, to see that there is plenty of depth to the ribcage, to complement the leg.

HINDQUARTERS

Many of today's Beardies are too straight in stifle, which in turn shortens the appearance of the dog. If the stifle is straight, so also is the shoulder, and so is the rib, and therefore the construction is incorrect for a Beardie and also gives a shortened 'Bobtail' appearance. The Standard asks for "low hocks", and these allow the dog to move forward with an economical stride, which can never be achieved with hocks that are too high.

FEET

The description of feet tallies in both the English and American Standards, and it is self-explanatory.

Dog 5 to 4 in length, showing good topline.

Bitch 6 to 4 in length, showing no rise over the withers, poor topline.

*Too square
in croup.*

*Too short in back,
poor topline, sharp
drop off at croup.*

Short muzzle, drop behind withers, too high croup, no depth of brisket, high on leg, Old English Sheepdog topline, insufficient bend of stifle.

TAIL

Surprisingly, there is not a description in the old Standard. This is a very important feature, being part of the working dog's balance and stopping mechanism.

GAIT

The Beardie is like the Border Collie: when on the move he should not be strung up on the very tight lead (as a terrier when on the move); it should be allowed to move with a loose lead, so that its natural, smooth, far-reaching gait is not impaired in any way. It is natural for its head to be either level with its back, or just slightly raised. The head should never pulled up so high that the dog short-steps, or hackneys. The topline must be level, and the tail should be level with the back, in order to give a balanced picture.

COAT

The coat on the Bearded Collie is universally a bone of contention. Both the American and English Standards state: "Length and density of hair sufficient to provide a protective coat and to enhance shape of dog, but not enough to obscure natural lines of body." However, the winning dogs and bitches sometimes have coats nearly reaching to the ground. Joyce once asked a lady how her bitch complied with the Standard, as its coat was long and silky, and the shape of the body could not be seen, and she answered: "If you lift the coat up you can see the shape of the body." This does not seem to be the true intention of the Breed Standard. The long, profuse coat is not always the correct texture. The outer coat should be: "flat, harsh, strong and shaggy". Yet there is very little evidence of the correct texture of coat in some of today's Beardies. If a Beardie has the correct coat texture, but it does not have the glamorous white Collie markings, it is often overlooked, and the more profusely white-marked dogs are put up in the winning line. Newcomers to the breed will be led to believe that that is what they should aim for. The English and the American Standards mention similar requirements, but the American Standard includes the point that the coat should fall naturally to either side, but must never be artificially parted. However, both Joyce and Pat have lost count of the number of times when they have been judging and have seen a dead straight parting from nose to tail, with not a hair out of place. Time has been spent carefully parting the coat, which is supposed to be in a natural parting. There are also those exhibitors who trim the beard and feet, and suggest that the hair has grown "naturally" in this way.

Beardie showing first-class hindquarters, with correct hocks and tail-set.

High set tail.

Am. and Can. Ch. Bendale Special Lady UD stepping out.

Am. and Can. Bendale Special Lady UD showing superb movement.   Chet Jezierski.

COLOUR

The American Standard does not include "born slate", but instead they stick to the colours mentioned in the English Standard such as "born black, brown, blue and fawn", which are the colours described by Mrs Willison in her book, *The Bearded Collie*. The latest habit of introducing the colour of the Beardie as 'slate' is very confusing. The breed has altered in many respects, but the colours the Beardie is born with have not altered. If the puppy is born a grey colour, it is a blue born puppy; black puppies are born black. There are many pedigrees now that give the colour 'slate', and they are incorrect. The American Standard states that the coat colour may lighten with maturity, but in the case of the born blue and the born fawn, the colour change is so slight that is hardly worth mentioning. The breeding of light colour to light colour in the born brown Beardie has produced a lot of Beardies that go nearly white and cream – a colour that was never seen in the early dogs and bitches. Those born brown that go terribly pale usually do retain a darker colour on their ears, and it is hoped by the owner that the dog will darken when adult. They are not to be confused with the born fawn that will stay fawn.

SIZE

This was formerly 20-24ins for males, with females 18ins plus, but this has now been replaced by: males 21-22ins, females 20-21ins. This original size difference between the sexes was decided by the work of the dog. Today, there is still a size difference, and recently there has been evidence of a wider variety in the sizes of the dogs and bitches – a few over-sized, but more

Ideal markings for the Bearded Collie.

Correct markings, although there is no white muzzle or collar.

Too much white which extends behind the shoulder.

Patchy markings, too much white on the stifle.

Uneven markings on face, patchy, and too much white on the back leg.

under-sized. When the dog is smaller than the bitch as they circle the show ring on the lap of honour, it makes a farce of the Breed Standard.

FAULTS

The English Breed Standard does not have a separate heading for 'Faults', and breed points listed as Faults in the old Standard ("thick round ribs, too rotund in body, too short in length, meagre short tail, narrow skull, too long or too short nose") have more impact if they are listed under a separate classification. Breeders would then be guided on the right path, knowing that other people would certainly notice if their dog or bitch had a fault which was mentioned in the Standard. The American Standard states that there should be no cosmetic alteration of the Beardies, and that is something that should be included in the English Standard.

Chapter Eight

COAT COLOUR

The colour in Bearded Collies is a fascinating subject, and it is well worth an in-depth study. It can be so confusing that even specialist judges of long standing cannot always tell at a glance what colour a Bearded Collie is when they are writing their critiques after judging the dogs. Bearded Collies undergo colour changes throughout their lives. In the case of born blue and born fawn this is confined to a slight change of shading, but that is enough to confuse a newcomer to the breed. In born blacks and born browns the changes are far more dramatic, and a dog could look completely different each time it changes its coat as it grows to maturity.

Bearded Collies carry the genes for two basic colours: black and brown. However, they also carry dilution factors, and therefore a diluted black appears as blue, and a diluted brown appears as fawn. The result is that Beardies appear in four colours: black, brown, blue and fawn, plus white markings, which are inherited separately. The situation is further complicated by the paling factor, which affects all four base colours in varying degrees. Some born black and born brown Bearded Collies start to pale from as early as six weeks of age. This is first seen around the eyes, on the hocks and on the front legs. The new colour starts from the roots of the outer coat and spreads, so that by the time the dog is a year old it may appear a light silver in the born black, and cream in the born brown. This is when it can be virtually impossible to distinguish born black from born blue, and born brown from born fawn. However, the pigmentation, most clearly seen in the nose and lip colour should give the clue. The colour of the ears is a good indication of what colour the adult will be after the first moult. If the ears are darker in colour than the main body of the coat, it is likely that further changes will occur, and the coat colour will darken by the second year, although in most cases it will retain some grey colouring, again to a varying degree. After a dog is three years of age there is very little change in the colour shading once the adult coat is established.

The majority of Beardies in the ring today are various shades of grey with black pigmentation, and the few black adults stand out against a background of grey dogs. Black is always a

A born black Beardie paling to grey, but retaining the dark ear colour indicating the dark grey colour the dog will be as an adult.

dominant colour, and even if a born black dog that has changed to grey is mated with a brown Beardie the resulting litter could be all-black. However, the inclusion of brown in the mating of sire and dam means that the born black puppies will usually dilute to grey as they mature. The born black that stays black throughout its life should produce black puppies that retain their dark colouring, with no drastic shading of grey, as long as it is mated to a born black that has black colouring in its ancestry. Of course, the puppies will have the usual white Collie markings; mating for black does not alter the amount of white on a dog, so long as both the sire and the dam have the correct amount of white markings. When breeding for a particular colour it is essential to follow some basic rules, and this will avoid problems with mis-marking, loss of pigmentation and eye colour. Mrs Willison of the Bothkennar Beardies stated that: born black could be mated to black, brown and fawn; brown (that stays brown) could be mated to black, brown and fawn; fawn should only be mated to black and dark brown, and blue should be mated only to black. If this advice is followed the breeder should obtain the results that are desired, without introducing any new problems to the breed.

Both Pat and Joyce share an interest in strong, dark-coloured Bearded Collies, which relates back to the original Bothkennar and Wishanger Beardies. Joyce was lucky enough to see some of this stock in the early sixties, and was very impressed with the unmistakable colours, and also the texture of the coat and the pigment, which could not be faulted. The perfect examples of dark-coloured Beardies were the the very dark brown Ch. Wishanger Cairnbahn, the gorgeous black-coated Ch. Bravo Of Bothkennar, and Ch. Edenborough Blue Bracken, for those who want blue in their breeding.

BORN BLACK

Born black Beardies predominate in the show ring. Ch. Davealux Royle Baron was born black, his ears and hocks went through a lighter grey, then the grey that he changed to as he became an adult remained unchanged until he passed away at the age of fifteen and a half years. This is the usual process. When Joyce was judging Bearded Collies in Norway in 1981, she came across Nor. Ch. Black Angie, a bitch with excellent dark colouring and black pigment. When she traced the pedigree back she was not at all surprised to find a Wishanger breeding back in the fifth generation. In fact, the black Wishanger Winter Berry is the sire five times in the bitch line. Many of the early Wishanger dogs were exported to Norway and Sweden, and because there was a very limited number of stud dogs available, there was a lot of in-breeding. Margit Hallesby of the Rosneskilens kennels, owned and exhibited many of the early Beardies, such as: Rosneskilens Lay, Grey, Raine, Beauty Girl and Peggy Jeanette, who dominated the show scene in the seventies. Swedish Ch. Danielle, sired by Wishanger Winter Berry out of Sw. Ch. Aweltin Lass, was another to pass on such strong colour and pigment that it was still perfect in the fifth generation descendants. Winter Berry was sired by Newtown Blackie (black) out of Bothkennar Briary Nan. Swedish Ch. Aweltin Lass was sired by Ridgeway Rob (black) out of Bremhill Betty.

In the early days of the breed in Britain, Mrs Justine Warren went to Scotland to purchase an outcross Bearded Collie, and she chose a handsome black and white dog, later registered as Tuftine Brigadier. He had no papers, but in those formative days the Kennel Club allowed breeders to register Bearded Collies in Class 2 after a Championship show judge had assessed the dog as a true member of the breed. When the dog had produced three generations that had been registered as pure-bred, it could be accepted on to the Class 1 register. As soon as Joyce saw Tuftine Brigadier she decided to use him at stud on one of her own bitches and to start a line with all his excellent qualities incorporated in it. Tuftine Brigadier did not excel in the show ring, and breeders in those early days were anxious go to stud dogs that had achieved their Championship titles. Sadly, this is also the case now, and many breeders are quite happy to overlook the excellent qualities of a dog, and go to a top winning dog instead, regardless of the fact that he might not produce his like. Tuftine Brigadier had been working sheep, and could not forget his training. When he was taken into the Obedience ring and told to sit and wait for the recall, he amused everyone by giving us a display of an excellent outrun, and circled the showground before returning to his irate owner. He was a wonderful character, who had many descendants with his excellent attributes, even though he was only used three or four times at stud. He was mated to a working Bredon bitch, owned by Betty Foster, to Mary Partridge's Ch. Wishanger Winter Harvest, sister of Ch. Wishanger Cairnbahn, and also to Justine's own bitch. When Tuftine Brigadier's blood was mixed with the old Bothkennar bloodlines, the gorgeous black colouring showed up, even after several generations of watered down colours. It would have been a wonderful match if Nor. Ch. Black Angie had been mated to Tuftine Brigadier. However, when she was mated to the dark brown Nor. Swed. Ch. Beagold Billy Brown, the colours were outstanding. Billy must have contributed the dark, dark brown to some of the pups,

Fenacre Wish Me Luck: born black (with tan points under tail and eyebrows) at four weeks.

Fenacre Wish Me Luck at six months.

Fenacre Wish me Luck at sixteen months.

A born black puppy that will stay black.

*Norwegian Ch.
Black Angie
showing excellent
dark colouring.*

and Angie gave other puppies her jet black colouring. The dark brown never faded throughout their lives as the puppies became adults, and the black puppies in the litter stayed black with no greying tinges in their coats. Descendants from that litter were not only of excellent colour, but they had the overall quality to match.

Sadly, this black colour that stays black has all but disappeared. If a dog or bitch is seen with its coat black and white as a adult, it stands out and is admired by all. By mating a black bitch to a silver or light-coloured dog, the colour will be watered down until only one or even no black puppies will show up in their descendants. The only way to retain black lines is to mate a dog to a bitch from black lines that have stayed black as adults. The pigment is black, the inside of the mouth is black, the eyes are dark brown and even the nails are black. The sad situation exists at the present time when born black Bearded Collies from mixed colour parents are called slate and even registered slate, which makes it very confusing. Other pedigrees have had colours in the litter registered as grey. Surely the colour that the puppies are born should be the colour registered, i.e. black, brown, blue or fawn. This would save a lot of confusion, as it is impossible to tell what colour the born slate or grey will be as an adult.

BORN BROWN

If you want to breed with a brown dog (retaining the dark colouring) it can be mated to black, brown and fawn coloured dogs. That handsome dark brown Ch. Wishanger Cairnbahn is the sire and grandfather of many of the dark brown Beardies – browns that continue to be dark brown throughout their lives, with no watering down of light and paling colours. Marilanz Amber Gleam was unmistakably Cairnbahn's son in colour and coat texture, as was Wishanger Cairngorrach, who was a Cairnbahn son mated to his sister, Ch. Wishanger Winter Harvest. She was born black and stayed dark grey throughout her life. Cairngorrach never paled in coat; when he was out of coat it was still dark brown with no light shading. Coming further up to date, Ch.

Davealex Royle Brigadier carried that same dark brown colour, and when mated to another dark brown, Osmart Bronze Pandora At Pepperland, he sired a complete brown litter. In this litter was Pepperland Pandemonium, and she was mated to strong Wishanger bloodlines, namely Wishanger Buttertubs Pass By Quinbury (born black, but as an adult he was grey with very little white markings). The litter had mixed colouring, and Mr and Mrs Lewis chose the brown and white dog who later became Ch. Pepperland Lyric John At Potterdale. Lyric John went through a very pale stage before he grew his lovely dark brown adult coat, and his brother, Pepperland Lyric Paul, carried the strong colouring and stayed black and white into his adult life. Cairnbahn's dam was Ch. Willowmead My Honey, another dark brown bitch, who contributed her excellent colouring to many of her offspring. Mr and Mrs Hawkins' Grizlinda Morning Monarch was from two brown parents, Lyric John and Blumberg French Wood At Grizlinda. As they came from strong brown breeding with excellent pigment, they also passed on their good colouring.

The born brown Bearded Collie, at the present time, goes from brown as a puppy through a pale cream stage, where it is nearly impossible to know whether it was born fawn or brown. It is only by looking at the slightly darker brown on the ears that is it possible to tell what shade it will end up. It is hard to tell how this paling has come about so drastically; indiscriminate colour breeding of silver to light brown, fawn to silver, blue to blue, or blue to light brown could be the answer. All these dilutions could be the reason why there are so many pale-coloured Beardies in the ring today – colours that would have been described as foreign to the breed, and therefore untypical and undesirable, many years ago.

There are so many of these light-colours in the ring now that it goes unnoticed. In the early days of the breed the dogs had such strong colours that the first silver-coated Beardie really stood out, and breeders were attracted to the dog that produced this type, with the coat glamorously long, if a little silky, and so the change began. In some instances browns were mated in order to get that pale type of glamour, and this sometimes resulted in light eyes and loss of pigment in some of the litter. Not all dark brown Beardies have good pigment. Ch. Wishanger

Born brown:
Fenacre Linnet at
eight weeks.

Fenacre Linnet at ten months.

Fenacre Linnet at three years.

Cairnbahn had a pink spot on his nose, quite late in life, and his son, Beagold Haresfoot Coffee, had a pink spot in exactly the same place. Some judges faulted this, although his pigment was very dark brown. He never went through a paling coat process; he was dark brown at birth, and when his coat was parted it went dark brown to the skin, and he retained this dark colour until he died. The experiment was made of mating dark brown to dark brown – and it worked, even though Mrs Willison of the Bothkennar Beardies was always reluctant to attempt this combination, as she had found a weakness in born brown Beardies (which she did not specify) and she believed that doubling up would bring it to the surface.

BORN BLUE

In the early days of the breed there was no problem with producing the correct standard colours. In fact, colour was one of the minor factors when planning a litter as there was such a shortage of stud dogs. The breeders in those early days were quite happy to accept whatever came along – so that many of the dogs were born black or born brown, with just one or two with the dilution of blue. One of first blue to emerge in the sixties was Miss Lynne Evans' Ch. Heathermead Handsome, who was a lovely shade of blue, and a very handsome dog overall. Unfortunately he had slight Hip Dysplasia, so Lynne withdrew him from stud. In Joyce's first litter from Ch. Beagold Ella to Wishanger Scots Fur, she had five all black and white puppies, with one dog puppy that had the most unusual colour that could only be described as powdery blue, right down to the skin. At this time there were so few blues in the breed, that many people had never

Adult born blue, with super coat and pigment.

heard of, or seen, the colour before. After breeding several blue puppies Joyce has discovered that they differ quite a lot. Some are born a silver grey-blue, others are so dark blue that it is hard to tell what they will be as adults. In the show ring today many judges have to make sure, when writing their critiques, that the dog is in fact blue as they suspected. The Beardies with blue coats do not seem to go through shade changes like the born black and born brown. The coat on the body, ears and legs remains very much the same, with no darker or lighter shading. The most outstanding blue/white dog was Shirley Holme's Ch. Edenborough Blue Bracken – it was never difficult to tell if Blue Bracken was born blue or grey. The grey dog that was born black can have shades of brown eyes. The born blue dog should, as the Standard states, have eyes to match coat, which is dove-grey blue, a super feature of the breed, with correct dark blue pigment. Some owners of blue born Beardies are surprised when they are faulted because the dogs' eyes are brown. How this comes about I do not know, but looking at some of the colour coats, there could be a mistake at birth in that the puppy could have been born black.

Ch. Blue Bonnie Of Bothkennar was the dam of that other famous and world-renowned dog, Ch. Osmart Bonnie Blue Braid. Mr and Mrs Prestidge's Deldrove Solomon At Padworth had a lovely shade of blue coat. He was sired by Australian Ch. Torwynd Atlas Serendipity At Padworth out of Deldrove Blue Cloud. It is obvious that the blue colouring came from Blue Cloud's sire, which was Ch. Benedict Morning Mist. Edenborough Shepherd's Joy came from two well-known blue dogs on the sire's and the dam's line, Ch. Osmart Bonnie Blue Braid and Ch. Edenborough Blue Bracken. Shirley Holmes was well-known for producing excellent coloured blue coats; her Ch. Edenborough Sweet Lord was line bred from Ch. Edenborough Blue Bracken with the inclusion of Ch. Osmart Bonnie Blue Braid.

FAWN COLOUR

Fawn is a dilution of brown, so fawn and light brown Beardies should never be mated together. The lovely fawn colour would be produced in the puppies, but the born brown could suffer with the dilution and a very wishy-washy colour could well result. Therefore fawns should only be mated to black and to very dark brown. Mrs McCallum's Ralentando Rainbow is now a veteran, but still retains the gorgeous fawn-coloured, correct textured coat. Another well-known fawn bitch is Mr and Mrs Fletcher's Ch. Romalia Rafaelle; her litter brother is a strongly marked black and white. Rafaelle is still the only fawn Champion; her sire was Mrs Barbara Iremonger's Ch. Sunbree Sorcerer. There are very few fawns of quality in the show ring today, and the true born fawn can be confused with the born brown that has paled. The fawn colour at birth is so attractive it can only be described as pink champagne colour. The fawn does not go through a paling colour: in fact, born fawn Beardies change very little when they become adults; even though the coat moults it does not shade into light and dark. The eyes matching the coat colour is a special feature of fawns, and would be considered too light in a born brown. The fawn coloured nose and pigment can also be much lighter than the colour for the born brown.

TRI COLOUR

There are one or two lines that regularly produce tri colours, either black, fawn and white, or brown, fawn and white. The third colour, fawn, usually disappears as the young Beardies lose

American Ch. Gladenmead Be Good: one of the few fawns to be shown successfully in the United States in recent years.   *John Ashbey.*

A tri-coloured puppy at fourteen weeks: note the tan marking above the eyes.

their first puppy coats. The fawn colour shows on the cheeks, eyebrows, on the legs and under the tail. When the fawn colour surrounds the eyes it changes to grey to match the born black coat (that has already changed to grey), or if it is a tri coloured brown puppy and the fawn is around the eyes, the fawn changes to whatever colour the brown coat changes to. Too much white surrounding the eyes is mismarking.

MISMARKING

The Breed Standard states "With or without Collie markings", and then goes on to say that white should not appear above the hocks and outside the hindleg. Also roots of white hair should not appear to extend behind the shoulder. Some lines produce a lot more white, like patches over the body. These pups should be sold as pets as they have all the excellent characteristics of the breed, but fashion decrees that they should not be shown. As all the Bearded Collies here and abroad stem from the same few dogs, there is every chance that any line could produce mismarks. However, it is important to bear in mind that there are so many faults that can be produced in a litter of any breed – such as overshot or undershot mouths, and deformities (cow hocks, bad fronts, a high-set tail that is held curled over the back) and inherited health problems, all of which are very difficult to eradicate from a breeding programme – that a cosmetic mismarking should not be viewed as a major disaster.

Many breeders choose to keep the most perfectly marked puppy in a litter for show: the one with a full white collar, white front legs and chest, white hind feet, a white tip to the tail, and

Mismarked black and white puppies.

most important of all, a white blaze covering the muzzle and sometimes reaching over the head to meet the collar. These markings are usually preferred in born black and born brown Beardies. The wealth of white does not always show when the brown is going through its paling stage, but so long as the coat returns to its darker shade, the contrast with the white markings is very attractive. If the colour of the coat remains a very wishy-washy light silver or light brown, the white markings just add to the overall colourless coat. Balanced markings do add to the overall picture of the Bearded Collie. A dog with one white foreleg, and one black foreleg with a white foot, gives the impression of incorrect balance as it moves towards the judge in the show ring. Markings in the wrong place can also make the dog look as though it is out at elbow. A very large white collar can make a dog look short in body, as it breaks up the outline. The white factor is inherited, so that any litter with mismarked puppies and correctly marked puppies would certainly be carrying the gene for mismarking from their sire and dam. It would be a great help if colours were included on pedigrees, and this would eliminate the possibility of incorrect pairing in future litters.

PIGMENTATION

Pigmentation on the puppies usually comes by the time the puppies are eight weeks of age. Puppies that are born black have a black nose, black eye-rims and black lips. For no understandable reason some Beardies retain excellent pigment up to the age of two, and then lose mouth pigment. In some cases the loss of pigment extends to the nose and the eye-rims. This could be an inherited fault; if so, it is usually permanent. A dog that is otherwise sound should not be shown with a drastic loss of pigment. All sorts of remedies are tried to correct this fault. In some cases it has been related to a vitamin deficiency, and there are several products on the market that might help this pigmentation loss. In one or two cases this has been successful, but when the problem occurs in some lines, there is no remedy.

Chapter Nine

THE BEARDIE
IN BRITAIN

THE EARLY ENTHUSIASTS

When Mrs Willison (Bothkennar) retired in 1963, Shirley Holmes (Edenborough) and Jenny Osborne (Osmart) both began their kennels by acquiring Ch. Bracken Boy Of Bothkennar and Blue Belle Of Bothkennar respectively. Jenny Osborne had her first Beardie from Mrs Willison, Blue Bonnie Of Bothkennar in December 1963. Both are actively engaged in Beardies to this day. Mrs Willison's kennelmaids, who were lucky enough to have seen the original Bothkennar stock, started their own kennels. The three ladies were: Jo Pickford (Penhallows), who was given Int. Ch. Bobby Of Bothkennar, who accompanied her when she went to live in South Africa for several years, before she returned to Great Britain and continued her show career; Jackie Tidmarsh (Tambora), who had Amberford Bracken as her first Beardie, and later on, when she worked with Mrs Anne Matthews, was able to acquire Bausant Of Bothkennar; and Barbara Iremonger (Sunbrees), who had her first dog, Ch. Sunbrees Magic Moments, born in August 1969, from Suzanne Moorhouse (Willowmead), was given her first Beardie when she was a child. In 1955 she acquired Ch. Wishanger Barberry Of Bothkennar from Mrs Willison, a litter-mate to Ch. Wishanger Barley Of Bothkennar.

Mr Green was one of the very early Bearded Collie owners; his prefix, Swalehall, has been taken over by John Stanbridge. His early dogs were John Scrope Of Swalehall and Swalehall Martha Scrope. Joyce (Beagold) had her first bitch Gayfield Moonlight in 1963, and her second bitch was Beagold Ella (later to become a Champion). Ella was sired by Ch. Bosky Glen Of Bothkennar out of Martha Scrope Of Swalehall. Joyce's first dog was Jayemji Derhue. Janet Martineau (Jayemji) had her first Beardie in 1962 and has always been a dedicated Obedience trainer. Mary Partridge (Wishanger) was given her first Beardie, Ch. Wishanger Barley Of

Ch. Willowmead Barberry Of Bothkennar (Ridgeway Bob – Bra' Tawny Of Bothkennar).

Ch. Wishanger Cairnbahn (Ch. Willowmead Barley Of Bothkennar – Willowmead My Honey).

Joyce Collis pictured at Crufts in 1963 with Ch. Beagold Ella and Gayfield Moonlight.

Bothkennar, by her parents, and then acquired her first bitch from Mr and Mrs Hicks (Multan). Jessica and Jennifer Of Multan are evident way back in many present-day pedigrees. Michelle Taffe (Heathermead) was the breeder of the first dog owned by Lynne Evans. This was Ch. Heathermead Handsome, a very good-looking blue dog.

In those early days Mrs Banks (Gayfield) had several Bothkennar dogs, but she failed to campaign any of her dogs to their titles. Betty Johnson bought Bond Of Bothkennar from Mrs Willison, and then bred Ch. Blue Bonnie Of Bothkennar, later owned by Jenny Osborne. Betty Foster (Bredon) had a working interest in the breed, and she bred Bredon Whisper, who was the foundation bitch for Nick Broadbridge (Sallen). To this day he is producing many of the dogs working on farms in Scotland. Bob Prestidge (Padworth) started with a Sallen bitch born in 1968.

Trudie Wheeler (Cannamoor) had different bloodlines to the Bothkennar dogs, and made up her first Champion in 1963. Cannamoor High Society, Cannamoor Cameroon and Cannamoor Bonnie were being shown quite extensively in the sixties. Jean and Derek Stopforth (Davealex) had their first dog from Jenny Osborne, Davealex Blaze Away at Osmart. Their famous litter from Marilanz Amber Gleam out of Ch. Cala Sona Western Isles Loch Aber produced Champions and CC winners. Roy and Diane Winwood (Rowdina) started with Wishanger Crabtree in 1965, and she later became a Champion. Maureen Reader (Tamevalley) started her kennel with Yealand Conrad in 1966. She bred the famous bitch Ch. Tamevalley Easter Song At Potterdale, who in her turn produced Champions. Jackie James (Charncroft) bred many well-known Champions. Her first bitch, Wishanger Spring Harvest, was from Mary Partridge. Jenni Wiggins (Scapafield) had that marvellous obedience Champion, Ob. Ch. Scapa as her first Beardie (Scapa was litter sister to Ch. Beagold Ella). Jenni was also interested in showing her dogs and has bred many Champions, mainly from the line of her foundation bitch, Ch. Osmart Black Lorraine. Diane Hale (Broadholme) had her first Beardie, Bobby's Girl Of Bothkennar, from Mrs Willison.

Jim Logan (Glengorm) had his foundation bitch Western Isle's Loch Eport in 1966. She was the dam of Glengorm Auld Clootie, who was such a pathfinder in Scotland, winning so many Any Variety classes before the days of Breed Classes. Trish Gilpin (Glenwhin) had her beautiful bitch Ch. Wishanger Waterfall in 1968. Fred Randall (Kimrand) had his first bitch from Wishanger kennels. The next bitch was Charncroft Country Lass. He was the breeder of the well-known Ch. Kimrand Simon.

These were some of the exhibitors and breeders in the years from 1960 to 1969, and most of the winning dogs in the show ring are descended from these lines. Just one dog was brought in with unknown parentage, before the Kennel Club refused to accept unregistered Beardies. That was Tuftine Brigadier, brought in by Justine Warren and mated to a Wishanger bitch Ch. Wishanger Winter Harvest. Both were born black. Tuftine Brigadier had a jet-black coat, so many of his descendants can still be seen producing this jet-black colour.

LATER EXHIBITORS AND BREEDERS

In 1975 Lesley Samuels mated her brown bitch, Pepperland Pandemonium, to Justine Warren's Buttertubs Pass By Quinbury (born-black). The resulting litter was a mixture of colours, but from this litter Janet and Mike Lewis (Potterdale) picked a brown puppy dog. He went through

Ch. Pepperland Lyric John At Pottendale: an outstanding dark brown dog.

many stages of shades during his Junior time, but eventually settled down to become the very handsome dark brown dog, Ch. Pepperland Lyric John at Potterdale. He was famous throughout the Beardie world, and many owners of bitches flocked to him. He was known as Winston in the kennels, and although he sired some super puppies to different bitches, he has never produced his duplicate. Even his black-and-white brother, Pepperland Lyric Paul, did not have his outstanding quality.

In 1970, Shirley Holme's Ch. Edenborough Blue Bracken was born, sired by Rowdina Grey Fella out of Blue Maggie From Osmart. He is still the CC record holder and will always be remembered as the most handsome, sweet-tempered, top-quality blue dog. Many of his children were exported, many have also graced British show rings. Blue Bracken won thirty-nine Challenge Certificates and twenty-three Reserve CCs. He was sire of Suzanne Moorhouse's Ch. Willowmead Perfect Lady, who won Best Bitch at Crufts three years in succession. Another blue-and-white dog that was used extensively at stud was Catherine Parker's Ch. Osmart Bonnie Blue Braid, sired by Ch. Bravo Of Bothkennar out of Ch. Blue Bonnie Of Bothkennar. Jenny Osborn piloted him to eleven CC wins, and he proved to be a very dominant sire and grandsire. He sired many Champions to different bitches, and they inherited the distinctive characteristics of their father. He had a strong influence on Ch. Brambledale Balthazar, Ch. Orora's Frank, Ch. Charncroft Cavalcade, and Ch. Banacek Moonlight Blue. His daughter, Ch. Osmart Blackthorn Of Moonhills, was the founder of Ch. Moonhills Midnight Treasure, Ch. Moonhills Country Gentleman, Ch. Moonhills Gold Digger, all from three different litters.

Chloe Of Blumberg was born in Joyce's Beagold kennels; her sire was Tina Batty's (Blumberg) Ch. Davealex Royle Brigadier, and her dam was Davealex Wee Caley. Chloe was

Ch. Edenborough Blue Bracken: the CC breed recordholder.

the pick of litter and was given to Tina in lieu of a stud fee. The breeding was carefully planned by Joyce, as she intended to mate the best bitch in the litter to her Ch. Davealex Royle Baron. Unfortunately, she could not keep the bitch. Chloe Of Blumberg was then mated to Ch. Brambledale Balthazar's son, Blumberg de Roos Erasmus. From this litter Janet Lewis chose Ch. Blumberg Hadriana At Potterdale. Several Champions came from Hadriana: Ch. Potterdale Philosopher, Ch. Potterdale Patch Of Blue, Ch. Potterdale Phoenix, Ch. Potterdale Conclusion, Ch. Potterdale Ptolemy and Ch. Potterdale Byron. Ch. Potterdale Philosopher was used extensively at stud. He was top Beardie in 1985. Bryony Harcourt-Brown (Orora) had top quality dogs. Her best-known must be Ch. Orora's Frank (Ch. Osmart Bonnie Blue Braid ex Ch. Mignonette Of Willowmead At Orora), who won a total of fifteen CCs. He also sired the famous Ch. Potterdale Classic Of Moonhills, who won Best in Show at Crufts in 1989. Ch. Potterdale Persuasion, Ch. Chriscaro Chrystal at Orora and Ch. Chriscaro Chianti were also sired by Frank.

It is an impossible task to list every dog and bitch that has produced top-quality puppies, but it is interesting to see that nearly all the Beardies known today have descended from the Bothkennar dogs, with only one or two exceptions. At one time there were just two dogs that were used extensively at stud, Ch. Bravo Of Bothkennar and Ch. Wishanger Cairnbahn, and this obviously had an effect on the breed. Today there are many more stud dogs to choose from, and, thankfully, responsible breeding programmes means that most stock is free from hereditary disorders.

BEARDED COLLIE WINNERS AT CRUFTS.

Mrs Willison's Ch. Beauty Queen Of Bothkennar was the first Beardie to win the CC and Best

Ch. Osmart Bonnie Blue Braid: this handsome blue and white dog was used extensively at stud.

Ch. Brambledale Balthazar: a son of Ch. Bonnie Blue Braid, and an important sire in his own right.

Ch. Bravo Of Bothkennar: Crufts Best of Breed winner in 1962, and a highly influential sire.

Ch. Tamevalley Easter Song Of Potterale.

Ch. Deedledee Carefree Rupert: reserve CC winner at Crufts, 1987.

of Breed at Crufts in 1959, the first time Challenge Certificates were on offer to the breed. Brother and sister won the CC and BOB in 1960: Ch. Wishanger Barley Of Bothkennar took Best of Breed, and Ch. Willowmead Barberry Of Bothkennar took the bitch CC. Ch. Benjie Of Bothkennar won Best of Breed for three years, 1961, 1963 and 1964, with his nephew, Ch. Bravo Of Bothkennar, taking over in 1962 and winning the CC and Best of Breed. Bravo's litter brother won the CC and Best of Breed in 1965.

In 1966 it was the turn of Ch. Wishanger Cairnbahn to win Best of Breed. In 1967 Ch. Broadholme Adorable took honours, and in 1968 it was Cairnbahn's daughter, Ch. Wishanger Crabtree. In 1969 Ch. Bracken Boy Of Bothkennar took honours, and in 1969 the first bitch who did not have her title, Chantala Corrie, won at Crufts, with Ch. Wishanger Cairnbahn winning the dog CC. That gorgeous brown daughter of Cairnbahn, Ch. Edelweiss Of Tambora, won in 1971. In 1972 it was the turn of Ch. Osmart Bonnie Blue Braid, and Ch. Edenborough Blue Bracken won in 1973 and 1974. In 1975 Ch. Brambledale Balthazaar won the CC and Best of Breed. Two bitches won the CC and Best of Breed in 1976 and 1977 – Ch. Mignonette Of

Ch. Wellknowe Crofter.

Ch. Wellknowe Hillscout.

Wellknowe Mountain Song: a promising newcomer, pictured at fourteen months.

*Ch. Willowmead
Super Honey.*

Ch. Farleycross Haymaker: By coincidence, his three CCs making him a Champion were awarded by Pat, Joyce and Joyce's partner Felix Cosme.

Willowmead At Orora and Ch. Penhallow's Pink Panther. Ch. Black Magic Of Willowmead won in 1978 and again in 1980, with Ch. Pepperland Lyric John At Potterdale winning in between in 1979.

In 1981 Ch. Kimrand Stargazer won the BOB with Ch. Pepperland Lyric John At Potterdale winning the dog CC. In 1982 Ch. Willowmead Star Attraction was Best of Breed, 1983 Ch. Tamevalley Easter Song At Potterdale took honours, and in 1984 it was Ch. Zorisan Chocolate Surprise At Kewella. The first CD Ex. winner at Crufts was Quinbury Stormdrifter At Runival in 1985. Ch. Tamevalley Easter Song At Potterdale again won in 1986. In 1987 Ch. Davealex Royle Bianco At Bruernish won the Best of Breed. In 1988 Ch. Orora's Frank broke the bitch domination, but the bitches came back again when Ch. Potterdale Classic Of Moonhill won CC, BOB, Group and Best in Show in 1989; Ch. Moonhill Coming Up Roses won BOB in 1990, and another bitch, Ch. Scapafield True Melody, won BOB in 1991,

Bearded Collie dogs have won nineteen of the Best of Breed titles at Crufts since CCs were on offer, with bitches only winning fourteen BOBs. Dogs took most of the BOBs in the early days, but bitches seem to be excellent contestants for the top honours recently, with Brenda White's Ch. Potterdale Classic Of Moonhill making history by being the first Bearded Collie to win Best in Show at Crufts. Ch. Edenborough Blue Bracken, and Ch. Charncroft Crusader were the only two dogs in those early days to win Best in Show at an all breed Championship Show.

Chapter Ten

THE BEARDIE
IN NORTH AMERICA

The first import of Bearded Collies to America was in the early fifties, when two Bothkennar bitches were bought by a farmer in Connecticut. Whether they were intended as working dogs or were bought as pets, is not known, and there is no further information relating to the two bitches. However, in 1962 Bonanza Of Bothkennar was exported to the United States, and this was the first of a series of imports from British kennels, which included dogs from Willowmead, Brambledale, Osmart, Edenborough, Beagold and Tambora. At this time Mr Richard Schneider came to England to buy three Beardies to use in advertisements for the newspapers and television. He gave assurances that the dogs would be found good homes after they had been used. He was true to his word, and one of the dogs, Am. and Can. Ch. Brambledale Blue Bonnet, went to Robert and Henrietta Lachman, and she became a multiple CC winner and the first Beardie to go Best in Show in America.

Joyce was first invited to judge in America in 1975 at the Sixth Annual Match for the Bearded Collie Club of America. At this time the Bearded Collie had not been accepted by the American Kennel Club, and Mr Bill Stifel, the club secretary, was there to assess the breed. It was a two-day meeting, and a symposium was held on the first day. Next day, Joyce arrived at the show venue early, to see station wagons and cars everywhere, unloading Beardies and equipment, show cases and baggage. One unusual feature was that most of the Beardies were resting and shut up in large wire cages. Little did she realise that this would catch on in Britain, and now, in the nineties, most of the English Beardie owners bring their dogs and bitches in the same kind of cages. The show was situated at Mount Kisco, New York, in a valley surrounded by tree-covered hills – a beautiful spot – and the temperature was in the nineties. All was ready; then a Scottish

Ch. Brambledale Beth: One of the early American Beardies, pictured in 1974.

Cauldbrae's Tunes Of Glory: Best in Show, Mount Kisco, 1975.

piper, in full regalia, led Joyce into the show, playing the haunting tune of *Amazing Grace*. The steward introduced Joyce and called the first class into the ring. For the first time she was confronted with thirteen-week-old puppy dogs, and expected to put them in order of merit. The pups all looked gorgeous, but Joyce soon realised that the owners expected the same treatment for their babes as the Open dog class. She was confronted with several puppy dogs that were not entire, and had to consult the President on the rules, and was told that she must decide whether to evaluate this as a minor or a major fault. As all these dogs were under one year, Joyce made it a minor fault for the very youngest, and judged accordingly. She was very impressed with the winning dog from the American-Bred Dog Class. The owners were Mr and Mrs Jozwiak and the dog was Cauldbrae's Tunes Of Glory. He was bred by Mr and Mrs Morrison out of two English imports – Knick Knack Of Tambora and the sire was Jonathan Brown Of Tambora. The dog had excellent white markings with a harsh black coat. His head and construction were excellent. The best adult bitch was the lovely feminine brown bitch Canamoor Honey Rose CD TD, handled by the owner, Mrs Virginia Parsons. The sire was Ch. Rowdina Rustler out of Wishanger Comb Honey. She was bred and exported by Mrs Trudi Wheeler. The winning puppy was American-bred, Cauldbrae Tangle Of The Isles, sired by Brambledale Benedict out of Cauldbrae Miss Holly. The owners were Mr and Mrs Morrison of the Cauldbrae affix, and the breeder was Mrs Pauline Broome. This pup was so similar to the best dog, that Joyce thought they must be close relations, which would not have been surprising as most of the dogs at the show could trace their pedigrees back to the very strong Brambledale lines. When Brambledale Balthazar was in any

Australian Ch. Beardie Bloody Mary: Best of Breed in 1980 at a Match organised by the Bearded Collie Club of Greater Cincinnati in 1980.

pedigree, there was every possibility that his excellent quality, coat and construction, would be noticeable in his descendants. He in his turn was the grandson of that famous black/white dog, Ch. Bravo Of Bothkennar. Joyce met many of the early Bearded Collie owners at that show in Mount Kisco. There was a great variety of types, as the imports had come from so many different kennels in England. In fact, the situation was not dissimilar in England in 1975, where there was a mixture of types in Bearded Collies, with breeders usually in-breeding and line breeding on their own stock, and very rarely going outside for stud work. So it was not surprising that the Beardies in America had not settled down at this early stage to look typical of

Am. Ch. Kimrand Drummer Boy At Beagold, who completed his Championship under Bob Forsyth in 1982.

Am. Ch. Crisch Midnight Braid: Winners Dog at the 1986 Bearded Collie Club of America's Specialty Show.

the breed. There was also a variety of colours: very strong colours in the born black and born brown, with a very few born blues or born fawns.

In 1976 Mr Lawrence M. Levy was made an Honorary Lifetime Member of the Bearded Collie Club of America in appreciation of his services to the breed and to the club. He provided the initiative in founding the club and served as its Founding President (1969-1972) and as a Director (1972-1976). Mr Thomas M. Davies was also made an Honorary Lifetime Member in appreciation of his services to the breed and to the club. He served for seven years as Director (1969-1970, 1971-1972) Treasurer (1970 - 1971) and President (1972 - 1976).

A number of breeders had an influence on the development of the Bearded Collie in the United States. They include: Don and Gail Millar (Gaymardon), Lori Warren (Brisles), Mr and Mrs Nootbar (Richlin), Mr and Mrs Morrison (Cauldbrae), Mr and Mrs Shannon (Arcadia), Mr and Mrs Schneider (Ha'penny), Mr and Mrs Levy (Heathglen), Mr and Mrs Blumiere (Tudor Lodge), Mr and Mrs Reinlieb (Knightsbridge), Mrs Ann Dolan (Glen Eire), Mrs Virginia

Am. Can. Ch. Ha'penny Moonshadow: 26 All Breed Best in Show wins, 126 Groups and 487 Best of Breeds to his credit.

Parsons (Braemoor), Miss Ramona de Vore (Kittyhawk), Mr Terricone (St. Andrews), Mr and Mrs Jozwiak (Snowberry), Mr and Mrs Davies (Dunwich), Mr Cordes (Chordahyar), Mr and Mrs Lachman (Crickets), and Mrs Kay Holmes (Windcache). These breeders first started exhibiting the Beardie before it was accepted by the American Kennel Club, and many have continued breeding and exhibiting their dogs throughout the years.

Joyce's next trip to the United States was in February 1980, when she was invited to judge a Match and speak at a seminar for the Bearded Collie Club of Greater Cincinnati. She was warned not to expect more than twenty-five entries, but she was delighted to receive an excellent entry of fifty-four dogs and bitches. A Parade of Champions was also scheduled, and a total of nineteen Beardies were entered for this. The Best of Breed adult was Mr and Mrs Masters' Australian Ch. Beardie Bloody Mary, sired by the famous Australian Ch. Calderlin Leal out of Australian Ch. Penreens Annie Laurie. She had only just been imported into the United States. Best Opposite Sex Adult was Mr and Mrs Slovisky's Richlin Diplomat Of Angus, sired by Ch. Edenborough Adventure out of Ch. Richlins Royal Shag. It was interesting to note that American breeding was becoming stronger, and many of the Beardies had American-bred parents, and the British imports appeared further down the pedigrees as grandsire and granddam.

The Beagold Kennels had exported a black and white bitch puppy to Mrs Joan Blumiere, when she was about three months old. 'Tiffany' did not have the glamorous white markings, admired by many Bearded Collie breeders, but she had the most excellent black coat with the correct texture, and her construction was excellent. She was sired by Ch. Edenborough Star Turn At Beagold out of Beagold Penny Royal. Her brother, the multiple CC winning Int. Ned. Ch.

Ch. Tudor Lodge's Walter Raleigh (Am. Can. Ch. Ha'penny Moonshadow – Am. Can. Ch. Tudor Lodge's Anne Boleyn).

Beagold Bruin Scott, was exported to Holland. He was the sire of Mike Larizza's American Ch. Copper Clarence At Beagold. Am. Can. Ch. Beagold Black Tiffany CD CDX matured into a lovely adult and she went on to produce many good quality puppies.

Joyce was invited to judge the Specialty for the Bearded Collie Club of America in August 1986. It was a two-day show and she received the magnificent entry of 298 top-quality dogs and bitches. Her Best of Breed winner was Ch. Willowmead Summer Magic, sired by Glenwhin Kinlockie out of Willowmead Touch Of Magic. This was an outstanding representative of the

Am. Can. Ch. Brigadoon Lady (Ch. Crisch Midnight Magic – Ch. Britannia Will O' Wisp) a multiple Group winner.

breed, not too overdone in coat, beautifully presented and handled to perfection. He flowed around the ring with a smooth but happy gait. He was owned by Ruth Colavacchio and Pam Gaffney. Winners Dog was Mrs Tuck's Ch. Crisch Midnight Braid (Ch. Crisch Midnight Bracken out of Ch. Beagold Black Tiffany). Both dog and bitch were carrying the strong black colour with dark eyes, and the correct type of weather-resistant coat. Reserve Best of Breed was awarded to Mr and Mr Carroll's Ch. Regal Manor's Sir Lancelot (Ch. Crisch Midnight Bracken out of Ch. Parcana The Sonsie Tyke). Best Opposite Sex was Shadowmist Promise Of Spring (Ch. Macmont Mackintosh out of Penstone Shadow Of Beth) owned by Mr and Mrs Hays. This was a lovely feminine, bitch who moved with a free-flowing gait.

By 1986 many newcomers had arrived in the breed. However, the overall quality was excellent, and presentation could not be faulted. At the same show the Bearded Collie Club of America held a Parade of Title Holders and Veterans. This magnificent parade involved 107 Bearded Collies, and many of the winning dogs and bitches go back to the Beardies that were shown in Britain, and some that had been shown in the British show ring when they were youngsters. Among the dogs and bitches in the parade was Ch. Alashaw's Saturday Night Special, who completed his Championship at just ten months of age. His sire was Joyce's Best of Breed winner, Ch. Willowmead Summer Magic, who was exported to America by Suzanne Moorhouse. Magic's sire was Glenwhin Kinlochale, who in his turn was by English Ch. Wishanger Cairnbahn out of Ch. Wishanger Waterfall. There were several of James and Dianne Shannon's Arcadia Champions in the parade: Ch. Arcadia's Brushed Bronze, Ch. Arcadia's Cotton-eyed Joe, Ch. Arcadia's Country Music HC, Ch. Arcadia's Family Tradition, all

Am. Ch. Bendale Sweeter Than Wine.

Am. Can Ch. Bendale Special Lady: multiple Best in Show winner.

Ch. Gladenmead Lake Isle Mist, owned by Stephen and Stacy Blau, bred by Paul and Susan Glatzer.   *Ashbey Photography.*

Am Ch. Gladenmead Bogie Be Good.

descending from their famous stud dog, Ch. Edenborough Happy Go Lucky ROM, sometimes on both sides of the pedigree. Other well-known Edenborough-bred dogs were also included. Patricia McDonald's Ch. Bosques Pampas Patty CD HC is a winner of multi Group placings, and also has an Obedience degree and Herding certificate. Both her parents come from British imports. Her sire, Ch. Heathglens's Jolly Oliver was sired by Am. Can. Ch. Willowferry Victor, who was exported to Mrs Barbara Blake in Canada. Her dam, Ch. Pepperland Liberty Belle was exported to America by Leslie Samuels. She was sired by Eng. Ch. Rowdina Rustler out of Pepperland Pandemonium (dam of Eng. Ch. Pepperland Lyric John At Potterdale). En. Am. Ch. Chauntella Limelight appeared in the pedigrees of several Beardies in the parade. This handsome, brown dog, owned and showed by Shirley Holmes, won a first at Crufts when judged by Joyce, before he was exported. Diane Brunner's Ch. Crisch Deja Vue At Brynwood, is also a natural sheep-herder. She is sired by Eng. Am. Ch. Chauntella Limelight out of Ch. Tudor Lodge Koala At Crisch (Am. Can. Eng. Ch. Edenborough Grey Shadow was her sire and Am. Can. Ch. Beagold Black Tiffany UD, TT, Sch. AD was her dam). Joyce's highly successful Ch. Davealex Royle Baron, (Brigadier's litter brother) mated a bitch, when he was just over nine months, and produced Davealex I Own Him. I Own Him was the sire of Davealex Legal Aide, whose many descendants went to the United States. Ch. Crisch Midnight Crystal Mist is the granddaughter of Eng. Ch. Blumberg Hadriana At Potterdale. Hadriana's dam was Chloe Of Blumberg, bred by Joyce and given to Tina Batty (Blumberg) in lieu of a stud fee. Hadriana went on to be one of the kennel's best foundation bitches. The American Bearded Collie is based on the best of British bloodlines, and fortunately the breed has gone from strength to strength as it has grown in popularity and the gene-pool has increased.

Robert Greitzer and Dick Schneider's Ch. Ha'Penny Moonshadow has the record win of 26 All Breed Best in Show, 126 Groups and 487 Best of Breed wins to his credit. His last Best of Breed was from the Veterans Class, at the Bearded Collie Club of America's Specialty 1990. The dog's owners are to be congratulated on Moonshadow's youthful appearance – he looks like a Beardie half his age. Michele Ritter with the Britannia affix, is owner, breeder and handler of the super Beardie, Am. and Can. Ch. Britannia Ticket To Ride, who has the distinction of being an All-Breed Best in Show winner and a multiple Group winner, again in 1990. Michele is the owner of Am. and Can. Ch. Bendale Special Lady UD, who is now a Veteran, and has been a Multiple Best in Show winner. The list of her other Britannia winning Beardies is highly impressive. Sue and Willie O'Brien's Ch. Samara Standing Ovation was campaigned in America by Nona Alberano and soon won his American title. He sired several litters while in America and has now returned to Great Britain. Bea and Kevin Swaka (Classical), imported a dog from the British Potterdale kennels, who is now Can. Am. Ch. Potterdale Double Image HC Can. Am. ROM. ROMI. He was judged by Miss Tomlinson from England and given Best of Breed at the National Capital Bearded Collie Club Specialty. Double Image was sired by Potterdale Anderson At Ramsgrove out of Ch. Blumberg Hadriana Of Potterdale. Mr and Mrs Shannon of the Arcadia affix are now campaigning Ch. Arcadia Steel Dust. One of their earlier Beardies was Ch. Edenborough Happy Go Lucky, who was the brother of Ch. Edenborough Star Turn At Beagold.

Ch. Shilstone Charlie Charcoal (Ch. Potterdale Conclusion out of Ch. Potterdale Serenade) was recently imported to America, and he has done extremely well in the show ring. He was Best of Breed at the 1989 National Specialty and Best of Breed at the 1990 Westminster Kennel Club Show. Bea and Kevin Sawka and Nona Albarano imported a puppy from Brenda White, and he gained his title at nine months and two days of age. This would be impossible to achieve in Britain. He is now Ch. Moonhills Classic Plus Signs, and was sired by Ch. Potterdale Philosopher out of Ch. Potterdale Classic Of Moonhill. Mrs Penny Hanigan's Ch. Brigadoon's Extra Special was Best of Breed at Westminster Kennel Club Championship Show, a very handsome dog with excellent presentation. Her lovely bitch, Am. and Can. Ch. Brigadoon's Magic Lady is another multiple Group winning bitch. Her sire is Ch. Crisch Midnight Magic out of Ch. Britannia Will O'Wisk. The great grandparents are a mixture of English and American breeding, and there are four colours in her background.

In 1991 Mrs Brenda White judged the Bearded Collie Club of America Specialty. She was impressed with the quality of the entries, and agreed that they were very similar to the Beardies in Britain. This was not surprising as she found that many were bred from British imported Beardies, and several had been bred in Britain and then exported to America and Canada. Brenda was delighted with the Best of Breed competition, although she admitted that the class took some sorting out, and she had to make some very close decisions. Best of Breed was Clark and Lewis's Ch. Coalacre Just Johnny, and Best Opposite Sex was McDonald's Ch. Britannia Love Me Do. Best of Winners was Bea Sawka's Classical Dreamfinder, described by Brenda as a rich brown, with excellent construction, and all the necessary requirements that made her a worthy Winners Bitch. Best Winners dog was Folendorf, Ritter, Colavecchio and Carter's Bendale Rave Reviews, described by Brenda as "a superb free flowing mover". His breeder, Ann Wilding must be very proud to have exported such a super dog. The American-bred Bitch Winner was Sihl and Widell's Caledonia's Wee Bit Of Clover, and the Dog Winner was Solymosy-Poole's Bearberry'a Tonapan.

The American breeders are fast catching up, with their successful breeding, and sensible imports, combining similar quality types with established lines. As British breeders have progressed, so have the Americans. Brenda remarked that some noticeable faults that she was not happy with were short backs and steep croups. In her critique on the Veteran bitch classes she mentioned that third and fourth would have been placed higher if they had been longer in body. The Breed Standard requires the Beardie to be a 'five to four ratio, slightly longer in bitches'. However, when the ratio is six to four, it sometimes results in a weak topline, and this can be noticed with the Beardies in Britain. Length is more noticeable when the croup is so steep that the back seems of endless proportions. Joyce did not notice this fault in the dogs that she judged when she was in the United States, and it is to be hoped that the British imports are not taking this fault across the Atlantic.

In the American system of judging the classes are divided by sex. The categories are:

Puppy: The dog should be at least six months old when entered at a points show. At large shows the entry will be split into six to nine months, and nine to twelve months.

Novice: This is a class for dogs and bitches that have won less than three blue ribbons and have not won any points. This would be at licensed shows.

American Bred: This class is open to any Bearded Collie of any age that is bred in the United States.

Bred by Exhibitor: Any dog owned or co-owned and handled by the breeder can be entered in this class.

Open: A class for mature dogs and bitches. This is the only class that an imported Beardie can be entered in.

Best of Breed: This class is for Champions only, and they compete with the best male and best female from other classes.

Non-regular classes are held at Specialty shows and include classes for Brace, Team, Veterans, brood bitch and stud dog. Futurities are offered at some Specialty shows for puppies that were nominated before birth. When the Group is judged, four dogs are placed, chosen from all the Best of Breed winners, whereas we only have two chosen. The Americans have six groups as well but they are called Sporting, Hound, Working, Terrier, Toy and Non Sporting. The Best in Show is chosen from the six Group winners. Only two Bearded Collies will take points toward a Championship at any one show. They are the Winners Dog and the Winners Bitch. The number of points awarded can range from zero to five and is determined by the number of Beardies of each sex that are entered on a given day. In order for a dog of any breed to become a Champion in the United States he must win a total of fifteen points. Two of these wins must be majors (three to five points awarded at a single show) and the majors must be won under two different judges. A dog that wins fifteen points without any majors will not be awarded a Championship and continues to show at non-major shows.

The presentation of the Beardies in America is outstanding; although the coat on some of the Beardies is long, it still gives the impression that it is of the correct texture. If there is plucking over the eyes, it is done expertly and does not look unnatural or give the dogs and bitches a harsh expression. If the feet are tidied, they are also done professionally, with no unmistakeable scissor cuts showing. The topline on many of the winning dogs and bitches is excellent, showing a good arch of neck to withers, and then on to a level back. A very gentle slope of croup gives the Beardie an excellent outline. The American exhibitors are also better at keeping their dogs' beards and whiskers snow-white. This is a problem for so many owners in England. We do not succeed as well in keeping our Beardies with unstained whiskers and beards, without feeding dry food and keeping the whiskers rolled up in crackers.

The English names are now even further back in their pedigrees, showing that the American breeders are succeeding with their own stock. One or two dogs and bitches have been imported recently, especially from the Moonhill Kennels. Ch. Potterdale Classic Of Moonhill's litter, which she whelped after winning Best in Show at Crufts, was a major attraction for those wishing to incorporate this bitch's lines in with their own breeding. American breeders are getting a great variety of colours in their Beardies, and the fawns and blues show good pigment.

CANADA

The Bearded Collie Club of Canada was recognised in 1970; in 1990, twenty years later, it had one hundred and fifty members. The advantage for both Canadian and American Bearded Collie breeders is the availabilty of a gene pool across the border. This is one reason why both sides have outstanding quality dogs and bitches. They also take advantage of sensible line breeding and outcrossing, which is used whenever necessary. In Britain we have found out to our cost that too much in-breeding can cause problems. That is the disadvanatge of being a small island, with quarantine laws which restrict our breeding programme. When English judges return from judging appointments in Canada and America they always remark on the excellent quality of dogs that they have had the pleasure to judge. The many British imports have been incorporated wisely with established stock, and have further enhanced the quality of the breed. In 1973 The Bearded Collie Club of Canada invited Jenny and Ken Osborn to judge a Match. This was such a popular move that sixty Beardies were entered, some owners travelling from America, and the furthest traveller came from Thunder Bay, about 1500 miles away, just to watch the Match. The joint decision of both judges was Leduc's Ch. Raggmopp First Affair.

In 1974 Jean and Thys Jagersma offered Ch. Lovelace Of Tambora (Jonathan Brown Of Tambora – Irish Lace Of Tambora) at stud. The dog was bred and exported by Jackie Tidmarsh. Jean also owned Ch. Misty Shadow Of Willowmead, and both dogs were certified clear of HD. Although several American Beardie owners took their Beardies into Canada to the shows in 1974, the dogs were not registered with the American Kennel Club. That meant they were not eligible for Canadian Kennel Club registration either, so the dogs were not eligible to enter Canadian Kennel Club events, and even if they had won points, they could not have been credited to them. Many complaints were received and secretaries had to check their entries before accepting them. Lynne Evans was invited to judge the Specialty Show at Kingston, Ontario in 1975. As Joyce was travelling across the Atlantic to judge in Mount Kisco the following week, the officers of the Club invited her as a guest to their show. She was very interested to watch the Parade of Champions and to see the dogs, mostly imported from Great Britain, and a few bred in Canada. Many of the exhibitors at that show then travelled to Mount Kisco, New York State where Joyce was to judge.

Mrs Barbara Blake registered her Colbara Kennels very early in the history of the breed in Canada. She imported several Beardies, but also bred her own puppies. Willowferry Victor was imported from Nancy Scott (England) and he soon became a Canadian, Bermudan and American Champion. He was used extensively at stud, and he sired many many descendants who also gained their titles. Another well-known import was Brambledale Boz, who gained several titles in double quick time when he arrived in Canada. Before he left England he had won enough points for his Junior Warrant, campaigned by his owner -breeder Lynne Evans. Boz died in 1986. Carol Gold was another pioneer in the breed. Her most notable Beardies were: Can. Ch. Wishanger Marsh Pimpernel CD and Can. Ch. Raggmopp Gaelin Image, a born black, excellent quality bitch. Carol imported a very handsome dog from Margaret Jackson (Banacek) who soon became Can. Ch. Banacek Fawn Fabric. He was the sire of Alice Clark's Can. Am. Ch. Bedlam's Go Get Em Garth, who won the Canadian Beardie Specialty in 1978. The judge was British breeder Trudi Wheeler. Alice Clark bought a young black puppy dog from Joyce in 1971, who eventually became Can. Ch. Beagold Mr. Kelly. His litter brother Beagold Mister Oliver was originally bought by Chris Wilson, but was later sent to K. Florence. The first Group winning Beardie was Ch. Misty Shadow Of Willowmead (Ch. Wishanger Cairnbahn – Ch. Broadholme Cindy Sue Of Willowmead) owned by Jean Jagersma and bred by Suzanne Moorhouse (England).

As soon as the Beardie was recognised in the USA, owners started taking their Beardies to and fro across the Canadian-American Border to gain the converted double titles. Now very few Beardies of quality do not have American and Canadian show titles; some are also Bermudan and Mexican Champions. The Bearded Collie Club of Michigan was formed in 1977, and at their celebration the following year seventy people with twenty-six Beardies attended a fun match. Several new names were added to the list of members. Cecile & Jean-Pierre Guerin

*Can. Ch. Beagold
Jason Blue
(Rodoando Dark
Forest At Beagold –
Beagold Silver Mist)
Owned by Mrs
Leslie Belfit,
Vancouver Island,
Canada.
BG Photography.*

registered their Beardies under the "de Lavrin" affix, and they campaigned Sir Cesar de Lauren. Later Kelly Canham (Cameron) and Dawn Boshart (Newhaven) combined forces and had a super litter from Ch. Newhaven Inspiration CD and Am. Can. Ch. Colbara Fiona Cameron Blue. The puppies had Scottish names, such as Cameron's Scotts Blu Belle, Cameron's Cairngorm, and Cameron's Black Douglas, a very even litter of top quality puppies that will no doubt be gaining their titles in the not too distant future.

Shilstone Choir Boy was exported from England to Holland where he gained many international titles. He was then sent to Canada and was used at stud. He mated Ch. Classical Silver Cloud and produced a first-class litter for Kevin and Bea Sawka, including the quality bitch Ch. Classical One And Only. Choir Boy added more titles to his already impressive array, and then returned to Holland. British breeder Brenda White has exported some excellent quality dogs to Canada, and all have gained their titles. They include: Ch. Moonhills Classic Plus Sighs (Ch. Potterdale Philosopher – Ch. Potterdale Classic Of Moonhill), who was sent to Bea and Kevin Sawka and Am. Can. Ch. Moonhill's Rose Sachet (Ch. Hecatie Hellraiser – Moonhill's English Rose). It is not surprising that Bea and Kevin Sawka, were again named as the top breed kennels in Canada in 1991. They have a whole list of top quality Beardies registered in their name. One particularly impressive bitch is Can. Am. Ch. Classical Star Baby HC, who was given Best of Breed by Jenny Osborn (Osmart). Brenda White also found this bitch exactly to her liking when she judged the BCCC National Specialty. Bea Sawka showed her handsome brown Classical Champagne Charlie when Joyce judged the BCCA Specialty in 1986, and she

Beagold Blue Jay, first in Germany and then exported to Canada.

gave him Reserve Winners dog from a huge entry. Bea also imported Can. Am. Ch. Potterdale Paris (Eng. Ch. Pepperland Lyric John At Potterdale – Eng. Ch. Blumberg Hadriana At Potterdale).

English judges seem to be very popular, and they are invited regularly to officiate in Canada. In 1990 Anne Wilding was honoured to judge at the first independent Specialty Bearded Collie Championship Show at Brantford, Ontario. Previous to this show all the Bearded Collie shows had been held in conjunction with other club shows. Ann found her Best in Show winner in Am. Ch. Classical Guess Who, from Bea Sawka's kennels. The well-known Amberlea kennels, owned by Jean Henderson, has won several firsts and a Group first with Can. Am. BDA Ch. Birkhills Ebony Dexter, and a Group fourth with his daughter Ch. Amberlea's Sheer Fascination. Dexter also won Veteran dog at the 1990 Specialty. Jean won Winners dog at the 1990 BCCA National Specialty with Can. Am. Ch. Amberlea's Midnight Special (Ch. Classical Shadow Dancer – Ch. Amberlea's Sheer Fascination).

Not only do the Bearded Collies in Canada grace the show ring, but many are working well in Obedience trials. Nikki Ryan is a very keen Obedience competitor, and one of her latest excellent workers is Kollybarb's Winnipeg Lonely Shepherd. In 1992 numbers of Beardies are steadily increasing, not only in quantity but in quality. Bea Sawka is already exporting Bearded Collies to Australia, and there could well come a time when British breeders will need to import from America and Canada.

Chapter Eleven

THE BEARDIE
IN EUROPE

Due to the careful selection of a quality nucleus sent to many countries by experienced British breeders, Beardies flourish in almost every country in the world. In some places they are still something of a rarity, but in many countries there is a established breeding stock producing top-quality Beardies. However, Britain, the original home of the Bearded Collie remains a major exporter, helping to strengthen or slightly alter existing bloodlines. The first exports were either direct offspring of Ch. Bravo Of Bothkennar and Ch. Blue Bonny Of Bothkennar, or their grandchildren. Therefore every country started off with the same original bloodlines as Britain. Today there are bloodlines, both ancient and modern, in all countries; there are now hundreds of Beardies carrying hundreds of prefixes, which makes identifying the family tree too difficult.

Both Pat and Joyce have sent Beardies abroad, and they always like to see their dogs again when they are on judging appointments, and most particularly they like to see any progeny. It is often apparent that some countries work under extreme difficulties in gaining access to the bloodlines that they require, which is rather similar to the early British breeders. However, in Britain today the choice of breeding stock is so wide and varied, and no stud dog is so inaccessible that a day's journey cannot bring you the bloodlines or features that you require. In a number of countries breeders have to abide by the very strict conditions set by their Kennel Clubs. Dogs must be vaccinated yearly for both rabies and the other problem diseases, and current certificates must be presented to the vet on entering a show. Some countries have restrictions on how to breed, when to breed, how many and which puppies to rear. In many places restriction is placed on how many dogs may be kept per household. In some places puppy sales will only be helped by the Beardie Breed Club if both parents have been shown and been graded excellent twice. Bloodlines in some countries are very similar, with almost no possibility of out-crossing. The quality of the imports sometimes leaves a lot to be desired, but by then the animal has been too costly to discard. As the breeders make an enormous effort to try and improve bloodlines and animals by importing a dog/bitch from the country of origin, surely it should be a matter of integrity that they are sent a good-quality animal to "fly the flag".

The judging system abroad is very different from Britain, as most countries have fewer classes and very high entry fees. In many places it is customary to write a critique of every dog and also to grade them. There are differing views on grading. Should you be kind and grade highly, or should you grade "as you see them"? Are you helping the breeding of that country by upgrading, or should you speak your mind and reveal the faults as you see them? It is, of course, only your opinion, but will it be helpful? Will the owner be annoyed or grateful if you point out that their show dog is just a pet and really has nothing to offer the breed? Will they accept that they would be foolhardy to use it in their future breeding programme as you can foresee problems that are insurmountable and that will be with them for years? Mostly that is why a British judge's opinion is sought, as he or she will know of, and have seen, the parentage behind their animals.

SCANDINAVIA

SWEDEN

A Swedish consul, working in Britain, returned to Sweden, taking with him the first Bearded Collie to enter Sweden. Little is known about the dog or where he came from. Barbro Finkelstein (Bellbreed) had her foundation bitch bred from a Rowdina parent, followed by Osmart, Briaridge and Glenwhin bloodlines. Maine Lund Olson had Jaymji Cluni (by Ch. Wishanger Cairnbahn) from Janet Martineau as her first, followed by Bracken Box from Osmart in 1967. Possibly the first litter bred in Sweden was at the Bifrost kennel of Elsa Svarstad.

The many Swedish visitors to Britain have improved the standard of handling and presentation in Sweden. Many have imported dogs and bitches, giving Sweden most of the bloodlines, both ancient and modern, and thereby having many top-quality animals to stand at stud. There are many good and clever breeders in Sweden, giving the country, as a whole, a wealth of typical Beardies. This has been achieved in spite of the stringent Kennel Club regulations. The Beardie breeders' enthusiasm and interest is intense, and they seem certain to go from strength to strength.

Joyce has judged in Sweden on a number of occasions, and has seen the development of a number of Bearded Collie kennels. Mrs Barbro Finkelstein (Bellbreeds) is well-known for her Beardies, including the highly successful Bellbreeds Princess Airloch, an International, Swedish, Finnish and Norwegian Champion. This good-quality brown bitch was sired by Int. Sw. Nor. Ch. Glenwhin King Airloch out of Sw. Nor. Ch. Blue Belle From Osmart. Mrs Maine Olssen (Farmarens) is a leading exhibitor and breeder, and she is a regular visitor to Britain. One of her bitches that really stood out was Int. Sw. Fin. Nor. Ch. Farmarens Emily Blue, (sired by Ch. Osmart Bonnie Blue Braid out of Int. Nor. Fin. Sw. Ch. Tanboras Penny Brown. The Farmaren dogs and bitches can be seen at most shows in Scandinavia. Mrs Carina Jackson (Woolpack) has retained the super coat on much of her breeding. Int. Sw. Fin. Ch. Woolpack Night Surprise (Int. Sw. Fin. Nor. Ch. Woolpacks Emperor out of Int. Sw. Fin. Nor. Ch. Woolpack April) is typical of the type she breeds. Mrs Anna Carlbaum (Blandings) has a top winning dog in Swed. Fin. Int. Ch. Blandings Quite Impressive. He is a handsome brown dog and has won thirteen CCs under

Int. Nord. Ch. Farmaren's Black Nightcap Nicholaij: top Beardie in Sweden in 1988. Sired by Ch. Wellknowe Crofter.

eleven different judges. 'Impy', as he is called, is sired by Nor. Fin. Ch. Dearbolt Birthday Boy out of Blandings Carmen. Bifrost is the affix of Mrs Alsa Edgren. Her winning black bitch, Int. Nor. Sw. Fin. Ch. Bifrost Baby Lotta, is sired by Int. Nor. Sw. Fin. Ch. Mystique Of Willowmead out of Bifrost Bien Aimie. Mr and Mrs Gustavsson have the winning black dog Int. Sw. Nor. Fin. Ch. Malinda's Mighty Miller (Sw.Ch. Trollflojtens Mahalia Jackson out of Sw. Ch. Braids Marty Maroon). Mrs Bovvin (Braids) bred Int. Sw. Nor. Fin. Ch. Braid's Maverick, a handsome fawn-coloured dog, sired by Sw. Ch. Artix Gambler out of Sw. Ch. Benedict Morning Sun. Nicholby's kennels are owned by Mr and Mrs Staav, and one of their top winning bitches was Sw. Ch. Nicholby's Anna Karenina, a very feminine black bitch sired by Sw. Ch. Edenborough Prince Charming out of Blandings Queen Of Hearts. This was from their first litter, and was their first Champion. Mrs Bjorklund used two Farmaren's Beardies, breeding Int. Nor. Sw. Fin. Ch. Farmarens Black Xo to Farmarens Brown Edelweiss to produce her quality black bitch, Int. Nor. Sw. Fin. Ch. Artix Elviria. Mrs Vrethammar (Trollflojtens) was very pleased with her Int. Nor. Sw. Fin. Ch. Trollflojtens Little Scherzo, sired by Farmarens Quantas out of Bifrost Bianca.

The Beardies that Joyce judged at the Uppsala Championship Show in May 1991 at Osterbybruk were mainly from these breeders, with one or two newcomers to the breed, and just a few imports from Britain. Best of Breed was Potterdale Selection, sired by Ch. Sammara Standing Ovation out of Potterdale Persuasion, a British import. He was a very handsome grey dog, with an excellent outline and good coat, well handled by that professional expert, Miss Lundell Olsson, who has trained and handled many of her mother's Bearded Collies over the years. Best Opposite Sex was Ellgren Ruth, a newcomer to the show world. This dark brown

A group of Beardies from the Malinnda's kennel

bitch brought back memories of the top-class Beardies seen in the Championship Show rings in the sixties onwards to 1975. She was a gorgeous character, with excellent quality, correct texture coat, wonderful dark brown, expressive eyes, and dark brown pigment. She moved with a superb flowing gait. Pat was invited to judge the Jubilee Championship Show of the Swedish Bearded Collie Club, held in June 1991, along with Joyce's partner, Felix Cosme. Felix was to judge the bitches and Pat was to judge the dogs. This Championship Show was held at Vaxjo in the south of Sweden. Best in show was Int. Nord. Ch. Farmarens Black Nightcap Nicholai. Previously the Beardies had been included in the classes at the big International Championship Shows, where all breeds were classified. This was a very important show as it was their first, and very successful it was too. The entry was good and the exhibitors enjoyed themselves, together with the two English judges officiating.

DENMARK
In 1971 the first male Beardie, Osmart Black Buccaneer, went to Helga Pederson, (Vigsbjerg). Joyce judged in Denmark in 1977 and noticed that a lot of in-breeding had taken place from the Ch. Osmart Black Buccaneer bloodlines. This handsome black and white dog had produced top-class Beardies in the first and second generation, but as more and more in-breeding took place the quality of the dogs and bitches had deteriorated. A new bloodline was needed, so Joyce sent over Beagold Porter Harvey to Mrs Alice Hindersgall. Porter Harvey's breeding was Swiss Ch. Hylas von de Elsternhoh out of Beagold Penny Royal. He was a black and white dog that would complement the gorgeous black and white dogs and bitches already in Denmark. Later two more Beardies were sent: Beagold Holly Nott (Ch. Edenborough Star Turn At Beagold out of Beagold

Int. Sw. Nor. Fin. Eng. Ch. Beagold David Blue with a son and daughter.

Henrietta Berkley) and litter brother Beagold Horatio Nelson. These two went to Mrs Suzanne Anderson in 1979. Breeders have since been able to take advantage of more varied bloodlines, and when Pat went to judge in Denmark in 1990 she was delighted to see so many lovely Beardies. The 'old' bloodlines were very much in evidence, with obvious Willowmead, Osmart, Orora, and later additions from Sammara, Beagold and Potterdale – all equally recognisable.

NORWAY

One of the top breeders in Norway was Mrs Tove Olsen, with the Twinklestar prefix. Mrs Olsen had been breeding Lhasa Apsos and Beardies for several years, and then bought Beagold Billy Brown from the Beagold kennels. He soon gained many titles and sired some very good puppies. Mrs Olsen then bought English Ch. Beagold David Blue, who was top dog all breeds in Scandinavia for one year. He also gained many more titles and sired Champions over there. Before David went to Norway he sired litters in Britain. Mrs Olsen bought a beautiful brown bitch called Copper Caley At Beagold, another with strong black breeding in her lines, and a third sired by David. Later she bought David's son, who became Int. Sw. Nor. Fin. Ch. Beagold Nikki Nort. When David had to retire into the veteran classes, Nikki Nort carried on the family's winning tradition. A son of Nikki Nort, Nor. Ch. Twinklestar Extra Special Mix, was exported to Britain and has been successfully campaigned by Mr and Mrs Kiff. Mrs Gunn Lynestead campaigns a very handsome dog from that breeding, Twinklestar Wild Snowstorm. Gunn also owns Nor. Ch. Black Angie, the most outstanding black Beardie that Joyce has ever seen. When mated to David Blue, she had that lovely dark bitch, Ch. Lady Di. Mr and Mrs Evanger of the Tsarina kennels are regular breeders and exhibitors, and they imported Kimrand Tartan Tiger

Int. Swed. Nor. Fin. Ch. Beagold Nikki Nort.

Multi Ch. Beagold Bruin Scott.

from Mr and Mrs Randall. Mrs. Hallesby of the Rosneskilen Kennels, has been breeding Bearded Collies for a long time in Ostfold, Norway. Her breeding goes back to the old Bothkennar dogs.

FINLAND

When Joyce was invited to judge in Finland in 1978 at the Finnish Bearded Collie Club Show, she was delighted to receive a good entry at the Helsinki venue. Her dog CC winner came from the junior class, and he was called 'Boffe'. He was a very nice silver grey dog, bred in Finland, a son of the Best of Breed winner Int. Nord. Ch. Mystique Of Willowmead, imported from the Willowmead kennels in England. Joyce later noticed that all the winning line-up was Finnish-bred. The junior bitch winners were mainly bred by Leena Pispala of the Hill Trails kennel. First was a very attractive black/white bitch called Hill Trails Black Dream (sired by Aslam out Hill Trails Black Amy). The bitch CC winner was called Arabella, bred in Finland and sired by Rowdina Rafferty out of Laihuen Misse. Best of Breed was Best in Show winner, the imported Int. Nord. Ch. Mystique Of Willowmead, who featured as the sire of many of the Beardies entered at the show. By coincidence, Joyce's partner Felix Cosme picked out a dog called 'Moses' to do a handling demonstration, only to discover that he was best of Breed and Best in Show winner Int. Nord. Ch. Mystique Of Willowmead. It was not surprising that they both had an eye for this very handsome International Champion. Joyce later noticed that many of the Beardies were descended from imports from Britain. Dogs and bitches could be traced back to

Int. Nord. Ch. Mystique Of Willowmead: a success in the show ring and an influential sire.

Rowdina, Willowmead, Tarskavaig, Briaridge, Osmart, Heathermead and Brambledale. Others were descended from Swedish and Norweigian breeding. At this time the borders were open between all the Scandinavian countries so dogs could travel to all the shows. Now Finland is isolated from Sweden and Norway because of rabies regualtions.

Both Joyce and Felix were invited to judge at the International Winter Dog Championship Show at Turku in January 1992. Joyce was judging Rough Collies and Shetland Sheepdogs, and Felix was judging Bearded Collies (Partacollies, as they are called in Finland) and Border Collies. The judging system in Finland is very different from the British system, and it can be quite hard to understand. However, the Finnish committee issued leaflets and held a special meeting to explain how the system worked.

The dog and bitch puppy classes (six to nine months) are judged and a critique is written, but no grading is made. The best puppy is picked and given a ribbon. This is followed by the junior class (nine to fifteen months); each dog is judged, a critique is written, and then the dogs are graded individually against the Breed Standard and awarded first, second and third. Those that are given an extra award – Very Highly Commended (VHC) – are allowed to compete for the CC. The same procedure is followed in the intermediate class (dogs from fifteen to twenty-four months), open class (dogs from twenty-four to seven years) and veteran class (seven years and over). The best dog is then judged and the line up includes all the dogs that have received the VHC ribbon. If the winner of this class is already a Champion, it is ineligible to receive the CC, and the honour goes to the next in line that is a non-Champion. The same procedure is then repeated for bitches. The CACIB and the Reserve CACIB is then awarded at the conclusion of the Best Dog and Best Bitch classes to Beardies over fifteen months of age that are not International Champions.

At Turku Felix gave Best Puppy to Fontaine Black Excaliber, who also won an honour prize. His half-sister was Fontaine Black Fancy, and she won the bitch class and was Best Opposite Sex. In the junior class Moonhills Hot On The Trails (sired by Eng. Ch. Moonhills Monkey Business out of Eng. Ch. Potterdale Classic Of Moonhill) won the CC, but was second to CACIB winner Hill Trails Black Lovelace. Reserve CACIB winner was Lawnlake Male Cup-A-Pie, sired by Ch. Deabolt Birthday Boy out of Laggan Black Leda. The bitch CACIB winner was Ch. Hill Trails Now Or Never, and the Reserve CACIB went to the imported Potterdale Anniversary (Eng. Ch. Potterdale Philosopher out of Gillaber Caledonia At Potterdale).

Felix was very pleased with the quality of the dogs and bitches, and he thought that the presentation was excellent. However, Felix, as a professional handler himself, was a little disappointed with the training and handling displayed by the owners of the Beardies. Looking at the breeding of the exhibits, there were some Swedish imports from the Woolpacks, Farmarens, Blandings, and Nickleby kennels. There were a few more from Britain, namely from the Geliland, Potterdale, Wellknowe and Sammara kennels. However, the majority of the entries were Finnish-bred, proving that breeders were breeding sensibly, using their own stock, with only a few imports incorporated in their already well established lines.

HOLLAND

The very first import was Loan Charm Of Willowmead, (from Susanne Moorhouse) in 1956, followed by Windmill Hill Wayfarer by Ridgeway Rob ex a 'Rob' daughter. The first litter was bred from this pair in 1959. Elderberry Of Tambora followed in 1967, Oliver Black Of Tambora in 1972, plus a dog of Sue Harrison's breeding; the only information is that he had her prefix, which was 'Haresfoot'. Beagold Tansy arrived in 1973. The Osmart kennels exported in 1974 and again in 1975, when Osmart Holly's Jingle Bell arrived to play a leading role. The Davealex kennels were sending good-quality animals, including Massette From Davealex in 1975. In 1976 Multi Champion Beagold Bruin Scot (by Ch. Edenborough Star Turn At Beagold) was sent to Ben Scholte (Seagull) and proved to be a cornerstone for that successful kennel. Pat saw him when he was eleven years old, and his qualities were still very obvious. He has left a legacy of excellent animals in Holland that carry his sound bloodlines and excellent type.

Holland has many experienced breeders and a host of good animals. There has been a succession of top show winners to keep them in the forefront of the show world. Multi Champion Shilstone Choir Boy was sent over by Caroline Nicholson, although at that time he was very much a gamble, as in Britain he was a very naughty youngster. However, Joop Hartman quickly schooled him and then exhibited him to top honours in many countries. He now resides in Canada. He is by Ch. Pepperland Lyric John At Potterdale ex Ch. Potterdale Serenade. Osmart bloodlines were the beginnings of Piet and Puck van der Meulen's (Lucky

Multi Ch. Osmarts Queenie's Lucky Number, sired by Ch. Wellknowe Shepherd Boy.

Numbers) kennel in the seventies, and they have had strings of winners. The imported Multi Champion Osmart Queenie's Lucky Number must have given them their biggest winner. He is by Ch. Wellknowe Shepherd Boy ex Osmart Queen Of Clubs. He has won top honours in many countries; he has also won CACs under British judges, including Janet Lewis (Potterdale), Rosie Hayward (Binbusy), Bryony Harcourt-Brown (Orora), Barbara Iremonger (Sunbrees), Jo Pickford (Penhallows), and Pat Jones (Wellknowe).

GERMANY

The first imports were from Trudi Wheeler (Cannamoor) and from there the breed progressed very slowly. Bothkennar, Willowmead, Osmart, Brambledale and Orora sent good Beardies to give a sound beginning, providing both show animals and breeding future generations. Many more kennels have sent dual-purpose dogs in the latter years. One of the best known dogs of today is Multi Champion Whistbrae Bounty Seeker, who was bought by Maria Westphal Giesenkirchen, to complement the Willowmead bloodlines that her V. Karthauser Hain Kennel was based around. Bred by the Stevens, this superb dog, with outstanding true Beardie movement and construction, has been a wonderful asset to both Germany and other neighbouring countries. Sired by Ch. Charncroft Cavalcade out of Ch. Charncroft Cloverbelle At Whistbrae (both parents were bred by Mrs Jacky James of the Charncroft kennels), these 'old' bloodlines offer a wealth of opportunity to breeders to see the Beardies of yesteryear.

Int. German Ch. Black Varnen vom Karthauser Hain.

SWITZERLAND

One of the top breeders in the seventies was Mrs Kurzebein with the Elsternhoh Bearded Collies. She had the handsome brown Swiss Ch. Fant von der Elsternhoh, representing a line that had been lost in Britain. His litter brother, Swiss Ch. Hylas von der Elsternhoh, was brought back to England by his owner Mrs Jeanne Trevisan, and used a few times at stud. Joyce mated her black bitch, Beagold Penny Royal, to him and in the litter was a very handsome solid black dog, Beagold Porter Harvey. Porter Harvey was mated to Justine Warren's black bitch, Quinbury Lochiel Fling, and with the combination of so many born black that stayed black in their lines, the pigment and the colour in many of their offspring was strong in all the litter.

SPAIN

Felix Cosme was invited to judge Bearded Collies and Border Collies at The Collie Club de Espana. This is a club that caters for the five Pastoral varieties: Shelties, Beardies, Rough, Smooth and Border Collies. The Rough Collie is firmly established in Spain; it is a very popular breed that lends itself very well to the Spanish way of life, and the quality at the show was very

Swiss Ch. Hylas von der Elsternhoh.

good. There were not so many Shelties and only one Smooth Collie. There were several very attractive Bearded Collies – in fact the Best in Show was a very glamorous, handsome grey Bearded Collie, beautifully presented and handled by a professional handler. The dog's name was Driver de Gouth Noire, sired by Ch. Shilstone Diplomat out of Ch. Tiffany's del Narciso.

The President of the club is Josephine Gomez Toldra, who is well-known in most of the countries on the Continent, as she is called upon every week to judge, mainly the pastoral breeds, but also other breeds in the Working Group. Josephine has been breeding Bearded Collies for nineteen years and her affix, Gran Kahn, features strongly in all the Champions that have been made up in Spain. Her first Bearded Collie was Creagmoir Xenophon. She made him a Champion in 1977, but sadly he was killed on the road. Her famous Ch. Davealex Royle Bronze was twelve months old when he started his career in the show ring, and he went on to win titles in France, Italy, Spain and Portugal, becoming an International Champion. When Josephine took Bronze to Italy, Senor Bernini was so impressed with the dog that he asked if he could use him at stud. Bronze was only used at stud three times, and his last mating was not planned. Josephine was changing him from one kennel to another when he caught a bitch in season. The result was eleven puppies in the litter, and five became International Champions! Bronze was retired when he was ten years old.

Chapter Twelve

THE BEARDIE
IN AUSTRALASIA

AUSTRALIA

The very first imports into Australia came from Britain. Keith Higgins imported Ch. Calderlin Leal, who was bred by Dorothy Lindsey and exported by Mr Bob Prestidge (Padworth). Shirley Holmes sent two bitches, Edenborough Queen Victoria and Edenborough Star Trek, and the male, Rushmoor Loyal Crusader (a son of Ch. Davealex Royle Brigadier). These four Beardies arrived at virtually the same time, and gave Australia a wonderful start in the breed. Crusader became the first Champion. Beardies from the Willowmead and Padworth kennels followed later. Bloodlines have since been enhanced by stock from the Tamevalley, Orora, Dearbolt, Binbusy, Potterdale and Beagold kennels. Some of the outstanding descendants that can trace their background to those early days are: Mr and Mrs Meredith's Aus. Ch. Sunnyspot Jade Angi (Ch. Calderlin Leal out of Ch. Noddfa Loch Maree), Ch. Tamevalley Highland Thistle, who was the sire of Aus. Ch. Meredale Wistful Lad, Aus. Ch. Meredale Wistful Lad and Aus. Ch. Meredale Winsome Lass. These dogs were all bred in New South Wales.

Mr and Mrs Smith (Burnhardt) imported Tamevalley Kindred Spirit (Ch. Potterdale Ptolemy out of Twilight Mist Over Tamevalley) from Maureen Reader. He is closely line-bred on Potterdale, and Mrs Smith is planning to mate him to their brown bitch Aus. Ch. Tamtarn Crescendo Sunset, hoping for an all-brown litter. Another recent import into Australia was Ch. Binbusy Crescendo, owned by Mr and Mrs Andrew. This dog has certainly made his presence felt as he is the sire of eleven Champions and six Best in Show winners from five litters. Trish and Phil Wall own the Hermosoperro Bearded Collies. In 1978 they imported Ch. Edenborough Vindicator and Banacek Miss Muffet. When this pair were mated they produced Aus. Ch. Lainesloch Laurel. Laurel was then mated to Ch. Anubis Alex, and the third generation was

*Aust. Ch.
Hopsack Of
Tambora.*

*Barshelay
Nova Scotia.*

A line-up from the Brigadoon kennels: (back, left to right) Brigadon Lucretia Bee, Ch. Grandonbri Charisma, (front, left to right) Bonnie Gills Gulliver, Ch. Grandobri Esmerelda, Brigadoon Briony and Brigadoon Leg's Diamond.

represented by Hermosoperro Hiska, sired by Burnhardt Sir Brutus. Their latest youngsters, both brown, are Hermosoperro Hot Toffee and Hermosoperro Heza Wina. They are producing a lovely type of Bearded Collie, and many good browns.

Keith Higgins was lucky enough to get the affix "Beardie". He owned the Dog CC and Best of Breed winner Beardie Blue Beard in 1977. Brian Dowse and Graham Kerr were very active breeders and exhibitors for many years. They won the Royal Easter Show with their UK import Ch. Kykencook's Diplomat in 1974, then again in 1979 with Ch. Anubis Lady Babette. The Anubis affix could be seen on many winning lists from then on. In 1976 Graham Kerr imported Deanfield Royle Dounane from the UK, sired by Davealex Blue Blazes out of Davealex Gorgeous Gussie. Gussie was a litter sister of Ch. Davealex Royle Baron, Ch. Devealex Royle Brigadier, Davealex Royle Amber, Davealex Royle Kincross, and the slate dog who went to Mrs Moira Morrison in America and became American and Canadian Ch. Davealex Larky McRory. Mr and Mrs Don Smith made up many Champions, namely Ch. Gaweke Don Kerrin, Ch. Gaweke Bonny Bracken, Ch. Gaweke Bonny Prince and Ch. Gaweke Glen Shaun. Shaun was a very handsome dark brown dog, and Joyce gave him the Reserve Best Dog award when she judged in New South Wales. His character and temperament were like the first Beardies, his coat was of excellent texture, and he had super dark brown pigment and eye colour. He reminded Joyce very much of Ch. Davealex Royle Brigadier. Mr and Mrs Don Bladon imported Edenborough Petra (Ch. Edenborough Blue Bracken out of Broadholme Christina). They also made up Ch. Anubis Ben Eiche to her title. This was a blue bitch by Ch. Beachcomber At

Aust. Ch. Beagold Donna Belle.

New Zealand Ch. Anubis Milton Dameral.

Deanfield out of Ch. Dykenook's Jane Ann Trot. Their slate dog from the UK was Lainesloch Laird (Ch. Edenborough Vindicator out of Banacek Miss Muffet).

Joyce's Australian tour ended with an invitation to judge the 10th Anniversary Championship Show for the Bearded Collie Club of Victoria, and she saw some magnificent, top-quality Beardies. Best in Show was Mr and Mrs Stoates' Ch. Collard Eastern Moon. Later she discovered that he was Australia's Top Winning Bearded Collie of all time – he certainly looked the part. He was sired by Aus. Ch. Tamevalley Highland Thistle out of Aus. Ch. Padworth Silver Maiden. Both sire and dam were imported from Britain. Reserve to Eastern Moon was Mr and Mrs Smith's Ch. Burnhardt Glen Logan (Ch. Binbusy Crescendo out of Ch. Burnhardt Lady Kellina). Best Bitch in Show was again Mr and Mrs Stoates' Ch. Potterdale Pandora (Pepperland Andy Panda At Ramsgrove out of Eng. Ch. Potterdale Prelude).

Although there were some very good dogs bred in Australia from Australian lines, the British imports that sired litters and were bred from, stood out in very excellent company. It made Joyce wonder if the wonderful weather, wide open spaces for exercise, and the owners' loving attention, gave the dogs and bitches just that extra bit of glamour. All the dogs she saw were in splendid coat and oozed healthy out-going temperaments, without being over-excitable.

NEW ZEALAND

Joyce saw some excellent quality Bearded Collies when she was judging in New Zealand. Many of the dedicated breeders have carefully bred to type, mainly from Willowmead lines. Mrs Betty Douglas (Roseburn) is one of the early breeders, combining good temperament and excellent construction in some very nice dogs and bitches. Correct texture coats could be seen in most of her dogs. Colin and Pam Douglas (no relation) had the very beautiful brown bitch NZ. Ch. Anubis Milton Demerel at the Waikato and District Collie Show in 1988, and Joyce made this bitch Best of Breed. In her critique she described the bitch as having "beautiful quality correct texture of coat. Outstanding head shape. Excellent pigment and eye colour. Sound in front and rear. Moved with a graceful, far reaching drive". Their young bitch puppy Llanddona Romenna was also very good and was soon made up to a Champion.

Many of the New Zealand Beardies have Australian ancestors, who in their turn were imported from Britain. Quite a few breeders exchange stock with the Australian Bearded Collie breeders. Many years ago Joyce exported three Beardies to New Zealand to the O'Maree Kennels, and she noticed that they were in the background pedigrees of several modern-day dogs. Titus Black At Beagold went to Mary Warren, who had already bought Beagold Georgette. Georgette soon gained her title, but also excelled in Obedience and gained many more qualifications. The other bitch who went to the O'Maree kennels was New Zealand Ch. Telbeth Lucy Mac Of Beagold. She was sired by Ch. Rowdina Rustler.

Chapter Thirteen

BREEDING

THE STUD DOG

Every kennel of repute is known for the strength of its stud team; two or three dogs that have continually produced their like in every litter are greatly treasured. It is of the utmost importance to choose stud dogs with the prepotency to produce their own good quality, and to a smaller degree, those of their immediate ancestors. A stud dog's influence on the breed should be thoroughly researched. If a dog has been used extensively at stud, there will be several of his offspring in the show ring, and they will have many of the excellent qualities that can immediately be recognised as having been inherited from the sire. A prepotent stud dog will show his type when mated to several different bitches. His reputation will then rely heavily on his progeny, and the best bitches need to be encouraged to have their litters from him, providing that they are compatible.

All the Bearded Collies from a large kennel might be carrying the same prefix, but it does not follow that the stud dogs are from the same strain. The term 'strain' is used when the dogs are related closely to each other. Many large kennels have different lines of Bearded Collies that only have similar ancestors seven or eight generations back, and these would have very little bearing on the resulting litters. The sire and dam each pass on 50 per cent: half the genes of any animal are identical with half of each parent. The grandparents' contribution of genes has a 25 per cent chance of being inherited by an individual in the litter, and so on, until the fraction of genes inherited is minimal. Most breeders prefer to line-breed to one outstanding dog, especially if he appears on both sides of the pedigree and many of his progeny have carried his outstanding qualities.

However, there are a number of breeders who will only use a stud dog that has been successful in the show ring, failing to take other more important criteria into account. Both Joyce and Pat agree that temperament is of the utmost importance in a stud dog, yet this is often overlooked in

Ch. Davealex Royle Baron: A very popular stud dog at the Beagold kennels, siring some 300 pups.

Ch. Chrancroft Cavalcade: One of the first Beardies to win Best in Show at an All Breeds Championship Show, and a leading sire for the Wellknowe kennels. Anne Roslin-Williams

pursuit of a top-winning dog. Bad temperament can be inherited, whether it be aggression to other dogs, nervousness, or a shy biter – and what use is bad temperament in either a show dog or a family pet?

It is not enough for a stud dog to have valuable bloodlines, to have won in the show ring, and to be of excellent type and temperament. Great care should be taken to ensure that no known hereditary factors are present in the stud dog. Joyce has all her potential stud dogs X-rayed to check for for Hip Dysplasia. It is also a sensible idea to have the eyes checked for Cataracts, Collie Eye Anomaly (CEA), and Progressive Retinal Atrophy (PRA) – although there are no known cases of PRA in Beardies according to the records of the breed panelists. It has been suggested that stud dogs should be licensed, in the same way that bulls and stallions are licensed. This would certainly help to ensure the quality of the stud dog, and it would eliminate animals of poor quality being used carelessly, which is never to the advantage of the breed.

All experienced breeders draw up their own breeding plans and work towards the type of dogs they want to produce, both in terms of looks and temperament. All kennels have their own objectives, and it is interesting to examine the breeding programmes at both the Beagold and Wellknowe kennels, as it highlights the time, planning, and patience that is required in order to produce top-quality stock.

At the Beagold kennels several Bearded Collies were used at stud, but Joyce was always working towards finding the ideal pair. She bought Davealex Royle Baron, and he came from very strong lines to Ch. Wishanger Cairnbahn. His sire was Marilanz Amber Gleam and his dam was Ch. Cala Sona Westernisles Loch Aber. Baron proved to be everything that she wanted in a stud dog, and was dominant to nearly every bitch he mated. His daughter came to be mated to one of her other dogs, and not one of them seemed interested in her. The owner wanted a litter so much that she suggested that they used Baron, the bitch's father. She promised that should any problems arise from this in-breeding, she would sell the resulting puppies as pets. Baron mated her in no time, and the litter could not have been more in-bred. However, the puppies were perfect in every respect, proving that the in-breeding did not produce any problems. As the puppies grew to adults they were very healthy, with good temperament, and showing excellent quality. They had no mouth problems, and no mismarking. In fact, Baron was the father of over three hundred puppies while at stud, and only once did Joyce hear of a mismarked puppy, and that was produced by a bitch that was sent on a long journey from the North of Scotland.

Soon after acquiring Baron, Joyce heard that the Edenborough kennels had a puppy for sale, sired by Ch. Edenborough Blue Bracken out of Davealex Dawn Reign. Dawn Reign was sired by Marilanz Amber Gleam out of Rowdina Peach Aboo. The connection of both dogs with Marilanz Amber Gleam was exactly what she was searching for. The sire of Baron was the grandsire of the puppy that she intended to buy. This was how Ch. Edenborough Star Turn At Beagold came to the kennels. Ch. Wishanger Cairnbahn featured three times in Star Turn's pedigree, and once in Baron's pedigree. However, Cairnbahn's sire featured twice in the pedigree, way back, admittedly, but enough to dominate the type Joyce wanted. This proved to be the case, and the puppies that came from both dogs, to so many bitches, were of excellent quality, and many Champions were produced, both in Britain and overseas. They all had super temperaments that earned them the qualification of the "Beagold Temperament".

Pat always puts all her breeding plans down on paper first, and then finalises the decision by watching and assessing the animals involved. She is always totally and brutally honest about their faults and virtues. One of the aims of her breeding programme has been to produce a top-class male sired by her stud dog, Ch. Charncroft Cavalcade. She had used Cavalcade on various bitches, and became aware that, on average, he produced better females than males. This suited Pat extremely well, and she built up a strong nucleus of Cavalcade's daughters that, when mated correctly, passed on their qualities in their litters. However, in order to breed the top-class male, Pat realised that she had to stabilise the type very solidly for at least two generations behind the looked-for male. The Wellknowe kennels have always followed a policy of line-breeding, in order to be consistent in producing top-quality animals. So Pat mated a Cavalcade daughter, Holly, to Ch. Wellknowe Shepherd Boy. Holly was one of Wellknowe's best work dogs, a big strapping bitch of superb construction and a calm temperament. This mating produced Ch. Wellknowe Crofter. He proved to be an ideal Beardie, easy to live with in any situation, and he produced puppies of excellent construction, superb movement and sensibility. Pat used Ch. Wellknowe Crofter on Edenborough Grace Darling (a Ch. Cavalcade daughter out of Ch Edenborough Amazing Grace) and the best of the resulting bitches was Wellknowe Flowing Stream. Two and a half years later, this bitch was mated back to Ch. Cavalcade, and from this litter emerged Ch. Wellknowe Hill Scout – the top-class male dog that Pat had been hoping and planning for. Scout is a more glamorous dog than is usual at the Wellknowe kennels, and that is a bonus in the variety rings of today. He won the Challenge Certificate at Crufts in 1989, beaten for Best of Breed by Ch. Potterdale Classic of Moonhills, who went on to Best in Show at Crufts in the same year. Scout is a popular stud dog, and his winning progeny bear a strong likeness to him.

When a kennel advertises a dog for stud work it is essential that the dog should be fit and healthy, eager to work, and well-trained, so that the mating goes ahead with a minimum of problems. The stud dog must be fed very carefully, with a fairly high protein diet, which can be altered at any time to keep him in good condition. Extreme care and attention must be paid to him at all times to ensure that the demands of his lifestyle can be met and that he always presents a picture of health and vitality. All visiting bitches should be swabbed as soon as they come into season. This should be done by a vet, if possible, and it ensures that there is no infection which could be passed on to the stud dog. It also serves the purpose of checking that the mating takes place on the correct day. Some years ago Pat almost lost a Champion dog because she failed to insist that a swab was taken. If you have a valuable dog, it must be protected from all possible risk of disease. The ideal stud dog is one that remains keen and active at his work, with a minimum of health problems. If a dog is well cared for, there is no reason why he should not continue siring puppies at the veteran stage and beyond.

THE BROOD BITCH

A good bitch will always be the mainstay of the kennels. Stud dogs can be used for their bloodlines and/or their qualities, but it is the brood bitch who is the cornerstone and represents the means of producing future generations. When mated to different studs she should always leave quality animals to follow on. When starting a breeding programme, it is essential to acquire the best bitch that you can afford or that you can persuade the breeder to sell. Ask questions, and listen to the breeder, who should know the bloodlines intimately and be in a position to help and advise. Go and see animals of similar breeding in the show ring, and look and learn. Take time to decide which path you want to follow. Too many novices want to advance too quickly – always remember that nothing good and lasting is ever acquired in a rush.

Ch. Tammevalley Easter Song At Potterdale, a brood bitch who produced several top-quality litters.

Your bitch is the foundation of your kennels – don't fall by the wayside for lack of patience and knowledge.

It is not necessary to breed a litter from your bitch to keep her healthy: it is a complete fallacy that a bitch must have a litter during her life – bitches can live happily to a ripe old age without ever having been mated. A bitch should be not be bred from unless she is in first-class condition, and a nervous bitch should never be bred from in the hope that it might correct a poor temperament. This was proved by a Bearded Collie bitch that was taken in by the rescue service several years ago. The bitch had had a terrible life, dominated by a German Shepherd dog – and a cat, judging from her badly scratched nose. She was wary and suspicious of people, and there was little improvement, even when she had been taken in to a home and treated with love and kindness. A vet suggested that she should be mated to bring out her maternal instinct. He thought that when she had her own puppies she would probably settle down. She had good bloodlines, and she was mated to a stud dog that tied in nicely with her pedigree. When she went into labour she was supervised and encouraged throughout until all her puppies were born. She was left for a few minutes, but almost immediately there were sounds of distress. The bitch was very agitated and would not settle, and when two of the puppies were removed it was discovered that the bitch had chewed off their legs. It appeared that the pain of the birth had made her remember the pain she had been put through in her previous home. Six puppies were born and only three survived. The bitch had to be held down to allow the puppies to suckle, and they had to be weaned at two weeks. The puppies grew to adulthood, but the bitch continued to be vicious with everyone, and so she had to be put down. However, if the owner is thrilled with the quality and health of the bitch, and the bitch has no outstanding faults, the owner may well decide to breed a litter in order to produce a puppy with all the qualities of the dam. A bitch should be two years old before she has her first litter, and she should be no older than four years of age. Mature bitches become very set in their ways, especially when they are kept as house pets. They become thoroughly domesticated, and it is unfair to put them through the rigours of whelping and nursing a litter when they have never developed a maternal instinct.

Before making the decision to breed with your bitch you should make an honest, objective assessment of her virtues and her faults. Her bloodlines should be studied to ascertain where her construction and temperament come from, and only then should the quest for the stud dog begin. The aim should be to produce a litter even better than the bitch herself, so the choice of the stud dog must be considered in depth. He must have all the good points that the bitch has, and none of her faults, even if they are minor (doubling up on minor faults could well result in major faults in the litter of pups). Any family failings that come to light when studying the pedigree of the bitch and the dog will be passed on to the puppies, so go right back to the seventh generation when you are researching bloodlines. A super bitch that has done a lot of winning in the show ring may still have one or two minor faults to pass on. The perfect animal has yet to be born, and everyone has their own idea of what is ideal. However, you must be certain in your own mind about the type of dog you are trying to produce, and then work towards that objective. The pedigree is obviously very important, but it is only as good as the animal itself. "I have a super bitch, her pedigree is as long as your arm", is an often heard remark, but it means absolutely nothing at all. It is the knowledge of the dogs and bitches in the pedigree that is going to be of value, so that it is possible to recognise dogs of a certain strain. Many of the older breeders will have stored information about the ancestors of many of the Beardies way back in the pedigrees, and most will be more than willing to pass on the information.

No doubt at least one stud dog will have particularly appealed to you, but the decision must be – will this male be suitable for the bitch? This must not be restricted to appearance: he must complement the bitch's bloodlines, and improve on any faults that she may have. The future generations should be of equal quality to the parents, and at best, they should be of even better quality. This then must be the object of all breeding, whether it is for a replacement, a new puppy to show, or another dog, or your first attempt at breeding. Whatever the reason, this must be a carefully thought out and planned operation.

Some stud dogs, used extensively, have never sired their like. Each time they mated to different bitches, the characteristics of the bitch have dominated the litter. This is a stud dog that should not be chosen if you wish to correct a weakness in your bitch. You should be able to recognise a number of characteristics in the sire's progeny, and whenever possible, the traits and type from the dog's grandsire and granddam should be evident. When you have decided on which stud dog you want to use, the next step is to talk to the stud dog owner, giving details of when the bitch is due in season and the likely date when she will be ready for mating. Ear-marking the correct day is sometimes a bone of contention, as many people do not know the correct day, because they missed the first signs of the bitch's season. At the Wellknowe kennels, the owners can leave their bitches from four or five days into the season, so the bitch can then be mated at least twice, at the correct time for her, and hopefully have the litter that had been planned.

There are many mistakes that a first-time breeder can make, unless they have gone to endless trouble to find out all that is necessary for the comfort of the bitch and her puppies. The bitch should be wormed before she is mated, and the owner should have some idea of whether the bitch comes into season regularly, every six months, nine months or once a year. As the time draws near there are many signs to watch for: other dogs become interested in the bitch, the bitch may squat to pass urine more frequently on her walks, and she may flirt with any dog that approaches, although she will not accept any closer advances. At this stage the bitch should be checked every day so that the first signs of a discharge can be noted. The season will usually last three weeks, although many Beardie bitches cycle every ten to twelve months, and the season could last longer than the predicted three weeks. It starts as a mucous discharge, and this is followed by a show of colour, which should be counted as the first day of her season. When the colour has almost finished (which could be as early as the eighth day or as late as the sixteenth or eighteenth day) the discharge changes from pink to almost clear-coloured, and then the bitch is usually ready for mating. At this stage the vulva will be soft and swollen. There could be some bitches who do not conform to the normal breeding cycle. A Beardie bitch that was mated on the ninth day of the season had a litter, and another bitch conceived after being mated on the twenty-first day. Another bitch had three litters, and accepted the dog with successful results on different days each time.

THE MATING

Ideally, a stud dog should be kept in a separate part of the kennels, right away from the bitches, so that he does not become excited every time he gets the scent of a bitch coming into season. It is also preferable if the stud dog does not have to go near the bitches' quarters when he is taken out for a mating or for exercise. Joyce starts a dog at stud as soon as he is over twelve months of age. Pat allows the male to mate one bitch when he is eight to nine months old, but then leaves an interval and the dog will be not be allowed to mate again until he is fourteen to fifteen months of age. The young, untried dog will need to be helped and encouraged to mount the bitch, and for the first few occasions it is important to use a proven brood bitch with a calm and steady disposition – the stud dog may get put off if his advances are met by a nervous bitch that might attack him. If human help is given at the beginning of a dog's stud career, he will both expect it and accept it at every mating. The only danger of this approach is that it can make a dog lazy. At the Beagold kennels Joyce remembers starting a young Bearded Collie off with his first mating by lifting him on to the bitch's back, and from then on, at every mating, he sat back expecting to be lifted on, before he would continue. This was complied with on the next three occasions, but help was refused the fourth time. The dog had to mount the bitch, or she would be taken away. Finally, his feelings must have conquered his laziness, and he did the whole mating on his own. From then on, he accepted the new situation, and he became a fine, well-trained stud dog.

A dog and bitch should never be left alone together, either to mate or when they are tied. A valuable stud dog could be injured or put off mating by a vicious bitch throwing herself about or biting. The bitch may be physically receptive, but some bitches, particularly if they are maidens, may growl and try to bite the dog. It is therefore preferable to muzzle the bitch, ignoring assurances from the owner that she would never bite. It is better to be safe than sorry, and most bitches will soon accept the muzzle.

The tie occurs when the dog's penis enters the bitch's vulva, and the gland in the penis swells to such an extent that when the bitch contracts her vulva, she is holding the penis so tightly that the dog is unable to withdraw. During the course of the tie, the dog ejaculates sperm into the bitch. The tie can last only a few minutes and the bitch can still have a litter. However, twenty minutes to half an hour is more common, and it can go on for as long as forty-five minutes. During the tie the dog will climb down from the bitch's back, so that they are standing back to back. Both the dog and the bitch should be held firmly, but gently, so they do not attempt to break free. There is no hard and fast rule that every bitch mated will produce a litter, regardless of length of tie. If it is not the correct time, there are still dogs that will mate, but no puppies will be produced. Successful mating will occur on the day when the bitch is discharging her ova to be fertilised by the dog's sperm. A bitch could have a false heat, and she might accept the dog, but there will be no ova to fertilise, so no puppies. The stud fee should be paid at the time of the first mating. A second mating is offered by some breeders, especially if the dog is unproven. If the bitch is brought back the next day, or the day after, the dog will recognise her and be stimulated to mate her again. Most breeders offer a free mating at the bitch's next season if no puppies are born, although the same stud dog might not be available. Many breeders would not want one of their show dogs to mate a bitch if it was the day before a Championship Show, as the dog will not have his mind on showing after this type of preparation!

If a stud dog is proving very popular at stud it is sensible to limit his stud work, for the safety and health of the dog himself. Some males are, of course, the perfect temperament for stud work, mating anything, any time, anywhere. They can always be relied upon to mate the visiting bitch. This ensures that the bitch's owner has not had a journey in vain. Sadly, some males are self-rationing and will almost require a prayer to St Jude before mating occurs. This situation can be exacerbated if the stud dog is expected to perform away from his home environment, although this is not always the case. Joyce recalls going to a show in the West Country with Ch. Davealex Royle Baron, and another breeder was anxious to use the opportunity to get her bitch mated. The Kennel Club rules that there must not be a mating within the grounds of the show, but she had made arrangements to go to a friend's house. They got in the car with both dogs and started the journey. Unfortunately, Baron smelt the bitch and made a lunge for her. Joyce could not hold him and the small car rocked with the tussle to hold him away from the bitch in the back. Eventually he broke his lead and proceeded to mate her. They pulled into a side road and were just in time to see Baron and the bitch tied. Joyce and the bitch's owner had to stand holding them for some fifteen minutes, deeply embarrassed as cars passed by!

Sometimes an owner wants to use a domesticated dog at stud, i.e. a dog that is kept in the house as a pet, and may even run with the other bitches in the house. This is not an ideal situation, as a young dog running with bitches will try to mount a bitch in play when she is not in season, and the owner will immediately chastise him as if he has done something wrong. If this happens often, the dog will be no good as a stud dog as he has been regularly warned not to mount a bitch. The dog should not be chastised, but distracted to another activity such as playing with a ball or his favourite toy, or being put out in the garden. A dog that is dominated by another will be very slow to mature, and might never have the inclination to mate a bitch.

BREEDING AND STUD TERMS

There are several ways of formulating breeding terms. When a bitch that ties in well with your breeding programme comes to your stud dog, it is quite usual to ask for a puppy in lieu of a stud fee, to carry on the line. All the terms should be written down, dated and signed by the recipient.

As time goes by it is easy to forget the details, so it should be stated in the terms whether you have first pick of litter, either dog or bitch. There might be only one bitch in the litter – then an agreement must be made with the owner of the dam so that there is no bad feeling. Right at the beginning all the details must be recorded in full.

The situation might arise where you have bought a bitch puppy, and paid less than it was worth because breeding terms are attached to your purchase. Again, all details must be understood by both parties. The bitch will not be mated until she is over two years old, and the person who chooses the stud dog, plus who pays the stud fee, should be agreed at the time of purchase. The owner will want either a dog or a bitch from the litter, or in some cases the breeder will demand the whole of the first litter. If this is understood right from the beginning, then it must be complied with. But all details should be written down, dated and signed by both parties.

A male can be sold for less money than he is worth, with stud terms agreed upon. For instance, the breeder will receive half the stud fee for a certain number of litters that the dog sires. All details should be discussed (such as services to missing bitches) and recorded. So long as the new owners are in agreement with the terms, there can be no misunderstanding later on. A dog sold under this type of arrangement might have to provide several stud services, or only one or two, and this should be stated in the terms. It is very unusual for a breeder to tie the buyer down for more than a few litters that the dog will sire, but it has happened.

Chapter Fourteen

WHELPING

After a bitch has been mated, she will need special care as she advances in her pregnancy. Diet needs to be considered, and today the scanning process has really helped to decide on the bitch's food regime. If you know that she is carrying a number of puppies, she will require more food that is high in quality, and if she is only carrying a couple of pups, you can avoid the pitfall of giving too much quality food and too many supplements, which results in enormous puppies, with the possibility of a bad whelping. If you do not want your bitch scanned and like to leave it to chance, there is no need to change her way of life for the first three or four weeks. She will expect to have her usual daily exercise and will eat the same amount of food. On the other hand, some bitches go through the stage where they refuse all food at the beginning of pregnancy, then eat everything they can get hold of as their time draws near.

It is usually around the fifth week that you start noticing differences in the shape of the bitch. Her teats look swollen, and she widens behind her rib cage. With maiden bitches it is sometimes very difficult to tell if they are in whelp, but bitches that have had a litter before, show all the signs of pregnancy and have been known to change in character. By this stage the bitch might also appreciate two meals a day, rather than one large one. Maintain her exercise, but as she thickens in shape she might prefer just a sedate walk.

As the time of whelping draws near, the bitch should have been installed in her whelping box, so that she has a chance to get used to it. It is a good idea to tack a blanket in part of the box, and use torn-up paper in the other half of the box, so that the paper can be changed as often as possible when the bitch is whelping. The box should have a pig rail running around the inside of it to prevent the bitch squashing the puppies behind her, and the pups also have a safe place if the bitch jumps in or out of the box too quickly. The whelping kennel should have some form of heat, such as an infra-red lamp. The telephone number of the vet should be firmly imprinted in your mind, and then all you can do is wait. The first signs that early labour is commencing is when the bitch starts to scratch around in the box, and she may ask to be let out frequently, in

Brown bitch with all black and white puppies.

order to pass urine. Make sure you accompany the bitch outside, just in case she has her first puppy outside. The first visible sign of imminent birth is when she strains and the water bag comes away. As each puppy is born, make sure it is dry and put it on a warm blanket, or in a box with low sides so that the bitch can see the pups; this will leave the bitch free to help another pup into the world. Most bitches will accept a drink of milk and glucose during the whelping and will eat the afterbirths. Some breeders do not like the bitch to eat more than one afterbirth, as it tends to result in diarrhoea. If the bitch has whelped a litter before, she will know exactly what to do. Fortunately, the maternal instinct is very strong in the Collie breeds, and so even if the bitch is a maiden she will soon settle down and allow the pups to suckle at her teats.

The bitch will spend a lot of time licking and cleaning up after each puppy is born, so much so that sometimes even when the pups have dried off, they become wet again with her constant licking. This usually happens when there is only a small litter, and so each puppy gets more than their fair share of attention. In a litter of over six pups, the first one has usually dried by the time she is ready to start off with her next round of washing! The litter should be watched closely to make sure that each pup is sucking well. There always seems to be one in the litter that falls off the teat and cries because it has lost its way and cannot get back. That one needs help for the first few hours.

After a short while, the bitch should be encouraged to leave the pups and go outside to relieve herself, even though she may be reluctant to go. While she is away, take up all the soiled paper and cover the whelping box with several sheets of clean, soft paper, and then some form of bedding can be tacked on top. You will have to be swift, as the bitch will hurry back to see what you have been doing with her litter. After whelping is completed give the bitch a light diet of

Blue bitch with a litter of mixed colours: blue and white, black and white and brown and white.

milk, fish and scrambled eggs. Make sure there is plenty of fresh water near her box, so that she can reach it without moving too far from her pups. After a day or two, increase her meals with plenty of nourishing food.

For the first two weeks the bitch and puppies should be contented, spending most of the time feeding and sleeping. However, there are danger signs to watch out for. There was a Beagold bitch who had a large litter, and she was doing very well – in fact too well. The poor bitch became very restless and wanted to leave her two-week-old litter. The vet was immediately called, and she was found to be suffering from eclampsia, which is a calcium deficiency. He gave her injections and after twenty-four hours she was back to normal. However, this condition can be fatal if it is not treated quickly. The bitch in question was such a good mother that she allowed her puppies to feed until she was drained of calcium. That is why a nursing bitch needs plenty of nourishing food, split into several meals a day. If possible, she should be fed before she settles down to suckle her puppies.

There was another occasion when a bitch had no problems with her litter until they were three weeks old. The pups started climbing out of the whelping box into the barricaded part, where the bitch went for a little peace, so the twelve inch high dividing fence was replaced with a fifteen inch fence. However, the litter, which had previously been quiet and contented, started to whine and cry. The bitch was checked and she was full of milk – in fact she was uncomfortably full. The pups were placed at her teats, and when they had fed they settled down to sleep. The bitch was then encouraged to return to her side of the barrier, but she would not jump – and this was the answer. She was the other side of the barrier when it was put up, and she had not attempted to jump over to feed her pups, although she had wanted to. She had been checked for Hip

Dysplasia and found to have a low score, so that was not the problem. It can only be imagined that she was lazy and considered that the barrier was put up so that she would not be allowed to get to her pups. This proves a point that a bitch and her litter should never be left for long periods. No one can ever tell when dealing with animals what may, or what can happen.

The puppies' nails should be cut regularly, as the puppies can scratch and make the bitch bleed with their sharp nails. It is no wonder that as the puppies get older the bitch first sits up to feed the pups, and then stands to feed the pups, and they have to reach up for a teat. Watch out for the smallest pup, who cannot reach, for this one will have to be put to the teat on its own. The Beardie bitch's coat should be cut before she has her pups. Cut the hair from around the teats, most of her tail feathering, and all the long hair on her back legs and around the vulva. This keeps her nice and clean, and also gives the pups clear access to the milk bar. The bitch should not be hurried back into the show ring, so that by the time she has grown a new coat she will have had a rest and improved her condition, especially if she has had a large, demanding litter.

Chapter Fifteen

REARING

The careful rearing of your chosen puppy is vital if he or she is to reach show ring potential. A good diet, and a regime of regular, controlled exercise must be adhered to throughout its growing period. However, whatever you hope to achieve with your dog, it must be reared correctly to ensure its future wellbeing. The puppy that is given the right physical care, socialisation and training will develop into the dog that you want. The choice is yours: it could include training for Working Trials, Agility or Obedience competitions, it could be a show dog or a pet dog, or indeed it could even fulfil its true purpose as a working sheepdog.

Today there are many schools of thought on what constitutes a good diet for a puppy. We have travelled a long way from the days when 'table-scraps' were considered sufficient, and there is a huge range of complete feeds or good quality canned meats on the market, as well as the more traditional method of feeding a diet of raw or cooked meat and biscuits. The option that you prefer may depend on what your adult dogs have thrived on, or you may be a novice owner and therefore rely on the advice of the breeder. Most dog owners have their own format for feeding, and most methods have their pros and cons. It is a matter of evaluating what suits your dog and your lifestyle.

At the Beagold kennels Joyce allows the bitch to stay away for long periods during the day when the litter is six weeks old. At this stage she increases the meals to five times a day: the first meal at 7.30am, the second meal at 11.30am, the third at 3.30pm, the fourth at 7.30pm, and the last meal at 11.30pm. Most bitches are quite happy to leave their puppies by now, and they will go back to their own kennel and adopt their own routine again, without so much as a backward glance. The puppies are wormed at five and seven weeks of age, and the new owners are advised to worm the puppy again after it has settled down in its new home. The puppies are fed in separate dishes, so that the amount each pup eats, or leaves, can be monitored. One or two might be slow eaters, therefore they are watched, so that the greedy ones do not oust them from their dish after devouring their own rations. Sometimes a reluctant feeder will eat more if it has competition, so another pup is allowed to share the dish, but a close watch is kept to make sure that the poor feeder eats the necessary amount. It is a good idea to feed at the same times every day, and then the puppies are looking forward to their meal; there seem to be fewer problems if they are fed to a strict routine. At the early stages drinking water is not left in the kennel. Water is offered several times a day, and then, later, water dishes are nailed to the wall, within their reach.

All puppies enjoy chewing, and hard dog biscuits or brown bread, baked in the oven until it is crisp, are good for their digestion and their teeth. Large marrow bones, which cannot splinter, are also beneficial if the puppies are properly supervised. The bones should be removed from the kennel every evening, and returned the following morning after they have been washed. Never leave bones overnight in the runs, especially if there are signs that rats or mice could be present, as they can contaminate the bones. At eight weeks of age the puppies should be on four meals a day, and although the number of meals has been reduced, the quantity of each feed is increased. The puppies are now ready to go to their new homes, and new owners are advised to feed three meat and meal, or biscuit meal, and one milk feed, which can be milk pudding or cereal with egg and milk.

At the Wellknowe kennels a different regime is adopted. The puppies are wormed at two weeks, and then started on warmed raw finely-chopped mince the following day. They are fed once a day for four days, increasing to twice a day for a further week. A milky breakfast, with porridge, is then started, making three meals a day. This diet is fed until the puppies are five weeks old when they are wormed for a second time. The mother is removed from her litter during the day at this stage, and allowed back at night until the puppies are six weeks of age. She is then taken away for three days, put back with her puppies for one more night, and the the litter is totally weaned. From five weeks onwards the puppies are fed a milky/cereal breakfast, a small quantity of complete dog food with canned puppy meat for lunch, raw meat for tea, and rice pudding at night. Initially, the puppies are fed on goat's milk, but by six weeks of age a dried powder is used. Pat considers that seven weeks is the least stressful age for a puppy to leave the kennels and adapt to a new home.

Most breeders of long standing have experimented with several different methods of feeding their puppies and adults, and they will have their own methods of feeding. At one time in Britain all types of meat were available at very low prices; tripe was in abundance, it was easy to buy ox-heads and liver from the slaughter houses, and the dogs thrived on this natural diet. It was unnecessary to rely on made-up complete feed, and there were few dog food manufacturers that offered anything for sale other than dog biscuits or deep frozen tripe in blocks. However, with the closure of abattoirs and the shortage of fresh meat suitable for dogs, many breeders opted to feed complete diets. At the Wellknowe kennel Pat still feeds a traditional diet of wholemeal biscuits and raw meat, and then she uses her own additives. The dog is a carnivore, and she believes that it should use its specially designed teeth to tear its meat. She argues that if the dog was intended to grind meals, such as those provided in a complete feed, it would have been given the necessary teeth to do the milling. However, she is prepared to accept that many people use complete foods for both quickness and availability, and if they have faith in that food regime, they generally achieve good results. The main objective is that the puppy achieves its physical potential. At the Beagold kennels Joyce feeds a small amount of meat with each meal of complete feed. This could be fresh meat or high-quality canned meat. The addition of natural food makes the food more appetising, and she very rarely has a poor feeder.

The two different methods of feeding at Beagold and Wellknowe, both equally successful,

A litter, fully weaned at six weeks of age.

A nice, evenly matched litter at eight weeks of age.

An puppy of Osmart breeding with a good head. Note that the puppy is teething and so the ears are unsteady.

show how important it is for the new owner to stick to the menu that the puppy is used to when it first arrives in its new home. There are so many different ways of feeding a puppy, all of which may be equally good, but if a puppy has to adapt to a new diet, along with all the other changes it is going to encounter in its new home, it is more than likely to result in the puppy getting an upset stomach. In fact, Pat recommends that the puppy should be kept on the breeder's diet for a minimum period of two weeks after it arrives in its new home. Both Pat and Joyce give all new owners a typed diet sheet, plus the pedigree paperwork, when the puppy is collected. Some breeders also supply an insurance certificate. Grooming is vital to the wellbeing of the Bearded Collie, and it is helpful if new owners can be shown the correct brushes and combs to use, and the breeder demonstrates how to groom the puppy, as well as showing how to check its eyes, ears and feet, and how to remove hair from the inside of the ears. Advice should also be given on caring for the coat in wet and dry conditions. The owner should be given the breeder's telephone number, so that contact can be made if a problem arises. Usually, these are just minor 'settling in' problems, and the breeder will be able to offer a solution. However, if it is anything more serious, owners should waste no time in contacting the vet. Most breeders are only too happy to give advice on rearing and training in the first few weeks, and they are always delighted to receive photographs and hear how their stock is progressing.

Puppies always seem to have enormous energy, but it is important to remember that they also need plenty of rest time. This is easier with kennel dogs, as they have longer nights and enforced rest periods during the day. They are also not subjected to all the hustle and bustle of a busy household. Some people keep the puppy in a wire crate for periods during the day so that it can see everything that is going on, and is out of harm's way. Once the puppy has rested, it can be let out to play.

As soon as a puppy has had its injections, which is usually around twelve weeks of age, the new owner usually has an overwhelming desire to take the pup out and show it off. However, this well meaning venture can do more harm than good. It is far better to restrict the outings to short trips, in the car to begin with, to get the puppy used to the outside world. If you try to rush things, you could end up with a nervous, frightened puppy. The puppy's exercise should also be restricted until it is six months of age. Freedom to run in the garden or compound throughout the day is ideal for the puppy to utilise the good food and build bone and muscle. It will rest when it is tired, and run about to play when it feels active. Young stock should also be allowed to run about on concrete, as this keeps the feet nice and tight. Continued exercise on grass is inclined to make the dog's feet spread.

By the time the puppy is six months of age it should be on two meals a day, and it should be happy to be exercised on a collar and lead, which will prepare it for its show career. The puppy should feel confident in itself before you attempt to take it to a dog training class or a handling class, and then when it has got used to the presence of other dogs and the noise (which must be tremendously stressful for a young pup) it can then be taken to a few small shows, just to have a look around. Let the puppy enjoy a relatively carefree youth, before any attempt is made to show it regularly. A puppy that is campaigned extensively from the age of six months will almost inevitably lose its *joie de vive* after a short time; the danger is that it will become a dull, uninterested animal in later life.

Chapter Sixteen

HEALTH CARE

The Bearded Collie is a healthy breed, and most will live to a ripe old age, with few problems other than loss of coat and general slowing up. Ch. Davealex Royle Baron had his injections when he was a puppy and never once was taken to the vet until he was put peacefully to sleep when he was fifteen and a half years old. However, daily care is essential to keep the Beardie in good health, and all dog owners should be observant and spot any signs of trouble before a major problem arises.

ANAL GLANDS
Some dogs suffer from blocked anal glands, and they will experience discomfort which they will try to relieve by sitting down and dragging their bodies along with their front legs. The best solution is to take the dog to the vet, who will empty the glands.

CAR SICKNESS
Many dogs suffer from car sickness, particularly in puppyhood. It is advisable to start off with a few short car journeys, and the dog will travel better if it is in a cage, lined with torn-up newspaper. Do not feed a dog before a journey, and hopefully, after a few journeys, the dog will get used to the sensation of travelling, and will settle down and go to sleep. If the problem persists, it is important that the owner is prepared to persevere, and does not give in, saying "I do not take my dog out in the car as he gets sick." One remedy is to put the dog in the car for a couple of hours a day, without moving it. Of course, this must be done in the winter, never in the heat of the summer. Travel sickness pills sometimes help, but patience is usually rewarded after several outings when the dog will enjoy the journey and your company.

CONSTIPATION
Dogs can become constipated when they have chewed too much on marrow bones. Once the dog

loses interest in the bone, it will have a normal motion. If it does not right itself, give a dose of Milk of Magnesia.

DIARRHOEA

Dogs should be fed separately so a check can be made on whether a dog is clearing its bowl, or leaving its food. If a dog is not eating and appears off-colour, check its motion. If it is the wrong colour, or there is diarrhoea, a course of vitamin B12 in liquid form usually helps the dog to regain its full fitness. Diarrhoea can be caused by over-eating rich and fatty foods. It can also be caused by an allergy to a certain type of food, such as milk, or it could be an emotional reason, such as fear from a thunderstorm. If you feed the same balanced diet every day, diarrhoea should be a rare occurrence. If a dog is suffering from it, feed boiled rice with soft-boiled eggs, or boiled fish, for a few days, and then go back to the usual diet. However, if the symptoms persist after a couple of days, the vet should be consulted.

EAR INFECTIONS

It is most important that the ears of the Bearded Collie are looked at regularly and the hair from inside the eardrum is removed as it grows. If the hair is allowed to stay in the ear it will form into a wad, and when this mixes with ear-wax, it forms a breeding ground for bacteria, and the ear will become inflamed. This problem can only be cured by an operation to open the ear to re-establish air circulation. If the hair is trimmed and the ear is cleaned regularly, using a weak solution of hydrogen peroxide on a cotton wadding, there should be no problems. If you are bathing your dog, make sure that no water gets into the ear; it is advisable to put cotton wadding into the ears before putting the dog into the bath.

FEET

Feet should be checked regularly, and the nails should be trimmed, if necessary. If you are washing your dog's feet, make sure you use medicated soap and water, and dry them thoroughly. If liquid soap is used it can make the nails too soft, and this can result in a fungus infection in the nails that is very hard to eradicate. A remedy is to soak the nails in iodine three times a day. If they are painful and soft, they will harden and dry with this treatment.

GRASS SEEDS

These can cause problems for dogs in the summer: they can get caught in their eyes, or in their paws, and they can cause a lot of trouble. When a Beardie has been out for a walk, give it a thorough check, from head to toe, to make sure it is free of thistles and grass seeds.

HEART DISEASE

This can affect a dog at any age, but it is far more likely to affect an older dog. The dog will tire easily, and will tend to cough and gag. However, if it is on medication from the vet, it will take life at its own pace, and enjoy pottering around the house and garden.

IMMUNISATION

Vets have differing views about the correct age to immunise against hard pad, distemper, parvovirus and leptospirosis. The most common practice is to take pups for their first injection at twelve weeks, then again at fourteen weeks. A puppy should not be exposed to any disease until